Speaking Effectively

Developing speaking skills for Business English

Jeremy Comfort
Pamela Rogerson
Trish Stott
& Derek Utley

CAMBRIDGE UNIVERSITY PRESS

Published by the Press Syndicate of the University of Cambridge
The Pitt Building, Trumpington Street, Cambridge CB2 1RP
40 West 20th Street, New York, NY 10011–4211, USA
10 Stamford Road, Oakleigh, Melbourne 3166, Australia

© Cambridge University Press 1994

First published 1994
Third printing 1996

Printed in Great Britain
by Scotprint Ltd, Musselburgh, Scotland

ISBN 0 521 37691 2 book
ISBN 0 521 37541 x cassette

Contents

Introduction to the learner   iv

Introduction to the teacher   v

Summary of unit contents   vi

Unit 1	Presenting information	1
Unit 2	Greeting friends and strangers	8
Unit 3	Explaining ideas and visual information	12
Unit 4	Phoning	18

Case study 1   21

Unit 5	Giving and getting product information	29
Unit 6	Small talk	33
Unit 7	Dealing with visitors	36
Unit 8	Offering help and Invitations	40

Case study 2   43

Unit 9	Meetings between colleagues	51
Unit 10	Arranging to meet	56
Unit 11	Informal negotiations	60
Unit 12	Developing a conversation	65
Unit 13	Chairing a meeting	68
Unit 14	Talking about people and places	73

Case study 3   77

Resource Section   86

Key   98

Introduction to the learner

Speaking Effectively develops your ability to communicate in English at work, both with colleagues and with clients and customers. It does this by looking at the most common areas of business communication, for example *Dealing with visitors* and *Phoning*, and by giving you the opportunity to practise the most important language in typical business situations.

Organisation of the book

There are 14 units and three case studies in the book. For a detailed look at what business communication situations and language areas the 14 units contain, please turn to the *Summary of unit contents* on page vi.

The three case studies give you the chance to use the language presented in the previous units, for example *Case study 1* focuses on the language presented in Units 1 to 4.

The cassette

There is a cassette to go with the book. The conversations on the cassette present the typical business situations and the important language as well as providing material for listening comprehension practice. In addition, in many of the units there are vocabulary pronunciation practice tasks on the cassette.
To use the book successfully it is necessary to work with the accompanying cassette.

The Key

The Key at the back of the book contains answers to all the tasks in the 14 units. Where there is no **one** right answer, a **model answer** is given. You may need to check your answers in these cases with a teacher or colleague.
The Key also contains the transcripts for all the recorded material on the cassette

Self-study

Speaking Effectively is primarily for use in class but the majority of the tasks in the units can be done on your own. However, the three case studies are more difficult to use if you are working on your own but provide useful reading comprehension and vocabulary development.

We hope that you enjoy using this book.

The authors

Introduction to the teacher

Speaking Effectively aims to develop the fluency and language competence of learners of Business English at the lower intermediate level. It does this by focusing on the most common business communication situations and by giving learners the opportunity to practise the typical language of those situations, both in controlled and freer speaking activities.

Organization of the book

There are 14 units and three case studies in the book. The odd numbered units are more business focused than the even numbered ones and are longer, containing four sections to the even numbered units' three sections.

In the odd numbered units the structure is this:
Language in context: learners are introduced to the main topic of the unit through a listening activity and/or discussion of photos and short texts, and are given the opportunity to relate the topic to their own experience and knowledge of the business world.
Language use: a close look at forms commonly used in business with practice tasks.
Business focus: specific areas of vocabulary are developed, with pronunciation practice in some of the units.
Role play: an opportunity to use the language presented and practised in a freer situation. In the majority of cases this requires using the information in the *Resource Section* at the back of the book.

And in the even numbered units:
Language in context: same as above.
Social language: a close look at forms used in social situations, with practice tasks.
Role play: same as above.

For a detailed look at the structure and organization of the units, please turn to the *Summary of contents* on page vi.

The three case studies give your learners the opportunity to recycle the language presented and practised in the immediately preceding units in interesting, motivating and credible business contexts. There are *Teacher's Notes* included with each of the three case studies.

The 14 units and three case studies have been developed in order of communication skill complexity with presentations coming first and external meetings towards the end. However, the units can be taken in any order in accordance with your learners' specific needs.

The cassette

The cassette, which is an integral part of the package, presents the typical business situations and the important language as well as providing material for listening comprehension practice. In addition, in many of the units there are vocabulary pronunciation practice tasks on the cassette.

The Key

The Key at the back of the book contains answers to all the tasks in the 14 units. **Model answers** are given where there is no one right answer. The Key also contains the transcripts for all the recorded material on the cassette.

Self-study

Speaking Effectively is primarily for use in class but the majority of the tasks in the units can be done by learners working on their own, so some guided self-study is possible.

Summary of unit contents

Unit 1 Presenting information

1.1 Language in context

Some features of good presentations
Listening — a business presentation

1.2 Language use

Describing organisations
Practice using *wh*-questions; *there is/ there are*
Signalling the structure of a presentation — introducing, sequencing and concluding a talk

1.3 Business focus

Vocabulary for describing different company structures and company hierarchy
Pronunciation practice

1.4 Role play

A company presentation

Unit 2 Greeting friends and strangers

2.1 Language in context

Introductions
Listening — conversation between old friends; introducing a stranger

2.2 Social Language

Practice of conversation starters and closers with friends and strangers

2.3 Role play

At a conference reception party

Unit 3 Explaining ideas and visual information

3.1 Language in context

Definitions of quality
Listening — a Quality Manager talks about his work

3.2 Language use

Explaining concepts and ideas — practice of simple language and step-by-step procedures to describe complex ideas
Explaining visual information — the language of increase/decrease applied to graphs and bar charts

3.3 Business focus

Vocabulary of quality management
Pronunciation practice

3.4 Role play

Presenting a work-related graph

Unit 4 Phoning

4.1 Language in context

The pattern of phone call conversations
Listening — a conversation between acquaintances

4.2 Social Language

Common telephone phrases and responses

4.3 Role play

Making a telephone call

Unit 5 Giving and getting product information

5.1 Language in context

The trade fair
Listening — sales talk at a sports equipment stand

5.2 Language use

Giving, getting and checking information

5.3 Business focus

Common business phrases
Pronunciation practice

5.4 Role play

A sports equipment buyer and a manufacturer's sales rep talk business

Unit 6 Small talk

6.1 Language in context

Topics for small talk
Listening — small talk among colleagues

6.2 Social Language

Giving encouragement: phrases for positive feedback; more emphatic adjectives and adverbs

6.3 Role play

Keeping the conversation going

Unit 7 Dealing with visitors

7.1 Language in context

Business visits
Listening — a tour of a factory in Italy

7.2 Language use

Giving facts, and explaining functions and processes
Asking for and clarifying information

7.3 Business focus

Using nouns and adjectives to form group nouns
Pronunciation practice

7.4 Role play

A factory tour

Unit 8 Offering help and Invitations

8.1 Language in context

Talking about eating out
Listening — lunch in the
factory canteen

8.2 Social Language

Phrases for offering and
accepting help and invitations

8.3 Role play

Entertaining a visitor in your
country

Unit 9 Meetings between colleagues

9.1 Language in context

Communication between
people at work
Listening — a meeting to
improve the efficiency of
internal communication

9.2 Language use

How to state your point, agree
and disagree
Practice of frequency, quantity
and number

9.3 Business focus

Different types of business
communication
Pronunciation practice

9.4 Role play

A short marketing
meeting

Unit 10 Arranging to meet

10.1 Language in context

Telephone terms
Listening — a phone
conversation arranging to meet

10.2 Social Language

Suggesting and agreeing times
and places

10.3 Role play

Negotiating to meet around
a busy schedule

Unit 11 Informal negotiations

11.1 Language in context

Considerations when
negotiating a deal
Listening — a credit card
salesman talks to the bank

11.2 Language use

Making conditions using the
present and future conditional
Phrases for stalling for time

11.3 Business focus

Manufacturing logistics and
distribution

11.4 Role play

Pairs or small groups
discuss the
implications of
problems at an
electronics factory

Unit 12 Developing a conversation

12.1 Language in context

Getting to know someone
Listening — a conversation
between business acquaintances

12.2 Social Language

Verb tenses in your life story

12.3 Role play

Finding out all you can about
a partner

Unit 13 Chairing a meeting

13.1 Language in context

The role of the 'chair'
Listening — a management
meeting about a recent
merger

13.2 Language use

Phrases for the chairperson

13.3 Business focus

People at work: their emotions,
skills and attitudes

13.4 Role play

Chairing and holding
meetings

Unit 14 Talking about people and places

14.1 Language in context

Talking about where you live
Listening — a conversation
about a town, a country and
its people

14.2 Social Language

Questions and responses for
talking about places and people

14.3 Role play

Pairwork on questions and
answers about places and
people

Acknowledgements

The co-authors would like to thank Trish Stott who worked long and hard to bring this book to fruition.

The authors and publishers would like to thank the following teachers and institutions for their help in piloting and commenting on the material:

Ian Clark, Universität Graz, Austria. Julie Rushden and Márcia Salazar at Britannia, Rio de Janeiro, Brazil. Ruth Lynch Delassus, Infop, Longvic, France. Jean-Paul Devaux, Josiah's Institute, Hong Kong. Jennifer Bovard at the Institute of Further & Continuing Education, Hong Kong. Karen Alen, Intercom, Madrid, Spain. Leslie Gruit, Dil Danismanlik Hizmetleri, Istanbul, Turkey. David Evans, Regent Capital Centre, London, UK.

The authors and publishers are grateful to the following illustrators and photographic sources:

Julia Bishop-Bailey: p.4. George Taylor: pp. 74, 81. Nigel Luckhurst: pp. 8, 12, 18, 29, 33, 40, 51, 56, 60, 65, 68.

Cover illustration by Richard Eckford.

Unit 1

Presenting information

1.1   Language in context

1.1.1

When you give a presentation, **how** you deliver the information is just as important as **what** you say. Knowing your subject well and knowing your audience are both very important for your preparation but there are other considerations. Below are some of the things to consider in order to make a good presentation – maybe you can add to them. Make a list of the features in your order of priority, then compare and discuss your list with the rest of the group.

body language	notes	language
confidence	voice	humour
speed	visual aids	length

1.1.2

Listen to a short presentation about a holiday tour company. It is being given to a small group of people who work for an advertising agency. How clear do you think the presentation is in terms of content and delivery?

	Clear	OK	Not clear
Content (What was said)			
Delivery (How it was said)			

1.1.**3**

[cassette icon] Listen to the presentation again and complete the data sheet.

Cultural Study Tours Data Sheet

Location:

    Head office: a) ....

    Branch office: b) ....

Company structure:

    Status: c) .... liability company

    Number of directors: d) ....

Responsibilities:

    Allan: e) ....

    Peter: f) ....

Number of staff:

          g) .... tour leaders

          h) 6 .... staff

Tour leaders' responsibilities:

          i) ...., The Russian Federation

          ...., ...

          ....

Administrative staff's responsibilities:

          j) ....

Company's activities:

          k) ....

1.2   Language use

1.2.1   Describing organisations

A Use the information in the presentation and in the organisation chart below to answer questions 1 to 6.

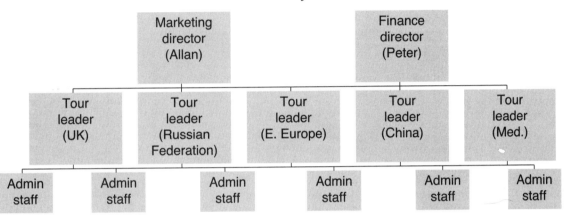

Cultural Study Tours

1 Who is in charge of marketing?
2 Who is responsible for the financial side?
3 Where is the company based?
4 What form of company is it?
5 Who is responsible for a particular region?
6 Who are the tour leaders supported by?

B **There is** and **there are** are often used in descriptions:
a) when talking about something or somebody for the first time, e.g.
There is a branch office in Edinburgh.
There are two directors.

But when we mention them again, we say:
It's in the centre of town.
They are responsible for finance and marketing.

b) When answering the question *how many?* e.g.
There's one tour leader for Great Britain.
There are eight of us in Head Office.

Look at the map showing the different sites of a company. In pairs, practise asking and answering questions about the sites and the number of employees they have. Use the map to help you, e.g.

How many training centres are there?
There's one. It's in Sophie Antipolis.

How many factories are there?
There are three. **They are** in Perpignan, Montpellier and Toulon.

How many employees are there in Marseille?
There are 52 altogether. 46 in the warehouse and 6 in the sales office.

Now continue.

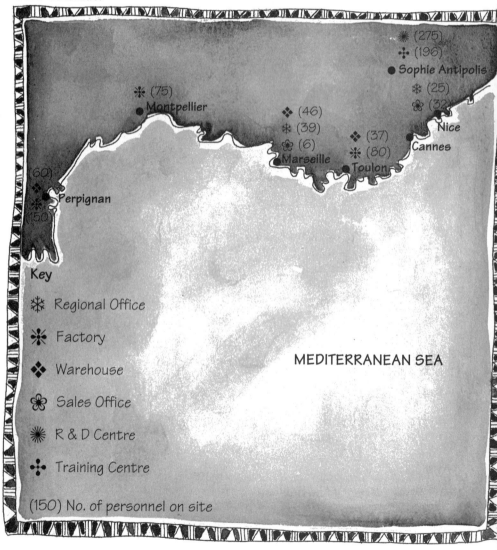

Key

❄ Regional Office

✳ Factory

◆ Warehouse

✿ Sales Office

✺ R & D Centre

✣ Training Centre

(150) No. of personnel on site

🖭 You can check your questions and answers with the models on the cassette.

1.2.**2** Signalling the structure of your presentation

Say what you are going to say.
Say it.
Say that you have said it.

A presentation will be much clearer to an audience if the structure is clearly signalled. Study the table below which gives examples of how you can structure your presentation.

Presentation Signals

Introduction

Topic	I'd like to talk to you about	our management
	I'd like to say a few words about	training scheme.
Outline	I'll be dealing with	
	I've divided my talk into	three areas.

Middle

Showing steps	First of all,	
	Firstly,	let's look at in-service training.
	Then	
	Next	I'll go on to external training.

Conclusion

Closing	Finally,	we hope to provide even more
	To sum up,	specialist courses next year.

Inviting questions

Are there any questions?
If there are any questions, I'll be happy to try to answer them.

Now prepare notes, and record an introduction and conclusion to one of the following topics:

- your company's holiday scheme
- flexitime
- a guide to your town or city

Listen to your recording, checking your *Presentation Signals* and your list of good presentation features.

1.3   **Business focus – Company organisation**

Study the following groups of words. All of the words in a group can be used to describe a particular aspect of company organisation. Add the words which appear in the box to one of the groups. Use a dictionary to check new words. The first answer has been done for you.

Location	head office main office _headquarters_	branch _subsidiary_......

Company status	limited liability co-operative incorporated	

Company structure	it consists of it is broken down into	division ....

People	director vice president the board	owner employer ....

Job description	managerial executive supervisory	

Job function	is responsible for is run by .... works with is involved in .... assists is responsible to	

supervisor	is in charge of	administrative
partnership	deals with	staff
subsidiary	reports to	clerical
headquarters	is made up of	manager
section	is divided into	employee
public limited company	department	

1.4   Role play

Now prepare and give a short presentation about your company or a company that you know. Try to use some of the language you have practised and some of the vocabulary from *Business focus*. During the talk, the audience or a partner should refer to the 'features of a good presentation' list discussed in 1.1.1.

Unit 2

Greeting friends and strangers

2.1 Language in context

2.1.1 Meeting and greeting

1 What do friends say to each other when they meet?
2 What do people say when they are introduced?
3 Which three topics do you think are most likely to follow in a conversation between two people who have just been introduced?

health	work
weather	family
recent activities	where you are from

2.1.2

Listen to the conversation between Allan Swales, his friend Jane Hallam and Peter Nicholson, a friend of Jane's.

1 Have Peter and Allan met before?
2 How does Jane greet Allan?
3 Which of the following topics do they talk about: food, work, weather, money, recent activities, clothes, health?
4 How does Jane introduce Peter?
5 How does Allan greet Peter?

2.2   **Social language**

Now look at the different ways you can make conversation with friends and strangers.

People you know already

	Beginning	**Replying**
Greetings	How are you?	Fine, thanks.
		I'm very well.
	How are things?	Not too bad.
Conversation starters	How's it going?	Great.
	Lovely weather!	Yes, it is.
	How's work?	OK/Fine/
		Not too bad.
	I haven't seen you for a while.	No, I've been busy/away.
Conversation closers	See you soon/ later.	Goodbye.
		Bye.
	I must be going.	See you soon.
	I'll be in touch.	Bye for now.

People you haven't met before

	Beginning	**Replying**
Introductions	May/Can I introduce myself/my colleague ...	Nice to meet you.
Greetings	How do you do?*	How do you do?
	Pleased to meet you.	Glad to meet you too.
Conversation starters	Have you been here long?	No, I've just arrived.
	Have you been here before?	No, this is my first visit.
	Lovely weather.	Yes, marvellous, isn't it?
Conversation closers	(I'm) glad/pleased to have met you.	(It's) nice to have met you too.
	It's been very interesting talking to you.	If you're ever in ...... you must get in touch.

*How do you do? is common in English and is usually combined with shaking hands, but only when you meet someone for the **first** time.

2.2.1   Complete the following dialogues.

A

Paul: .... Chris: .... you?
Chris: Fine thanks, Paul. .... you?
Paul: ....
Chris: I .... while.
Paul: No, ... busy, I'm afraid. In fact, I ....
         .... going.
Chris: OK, I'll ....
Paul: Right. ....

B

Jill: Pat, ... introduce .... Graham,
               Graham Murphy? Graham, ... Pat White,
               she's an accountant with ICN.
Graham: .... ?
Pat: ....
Graham: .... in Montreal long?
Pat: No, I .... yesterday.
Graham: .... city, isn't it?
Pat: Yes, ...
Graham: Well, ... nice .... you.
Pat: Yes, ...

Now listen to the model dialogues on the cassette and practise them with a partner.

2.2.2   Listen to the instructions on the cassette and decide what you would say. Speak after the tone. Here is an example.

You meet someone for the first time. You have talked to him/her on the phone. *I'm pleased to meet you.*

2.3   **Role play**

Situation

You are at a conference reception. Some of the people there are your friends and some are strangers. You each have a business card to identify yourself. (See Resource Section on page 90.) Talk to as many people as possible in the next five minutes.

Make sure you cover the following points:

1 introduce yourself
2 greet the person
3 start a conversation
4 close the conversation
5 introduce the stranger to a colleague of yours if possible

Unit 3

Explaining ideas and visual information

3.1 Language in context

3.1.1 Defining quality

Quality is about achieving excellence in a product or service.	Quality is the ability of a service or product to satisfy a given need.

Which statement do you agree with most? Compare your opinions with those of other learners.

3.1.2

Listen to this interview with Dr Clive Farmer of Rowburys, a leading manufacturer of chocolate and confectionery. He is talking about quality management. Which of the two statements about quality do you think he agrees with?

3.1.**3**

A Below are the four main areas of Dr Farmer's talk. Put them in the order in which he mentions them.

Area   **Order**
Describing visual information
Defining the company's aims
Describing his job
Calculating quality costs

B How clearly does Dr Farmer explain the aims of his company in terms of quality? Listen to the **first part** of the interview again and complete his definition.

The aim is to get people to ....

....

....

in such a way as to make a profit.

C How clearly does Dr Farmer describe the visual information in the *Optimum Quality Cost Model*? Listen to the **second part** of the interview again and complete the graph.

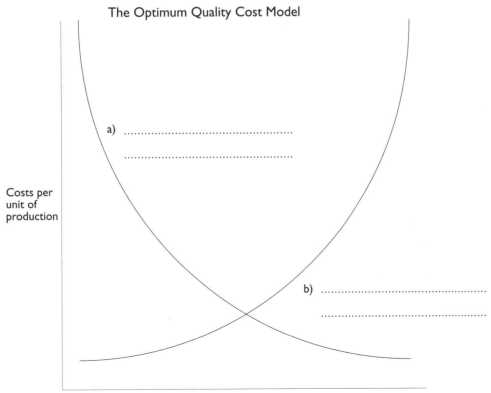

The Optimum Quality Cost Model

a) ....

....

Costs per unit of production

b) ....

....

% Defective products

3.2 Language use – Explaining concepts and ideas

You do not need complex language to explain complex ideas but you do need clear, well-structured speech.

3.2.1 Total Quality Management

Read the paragraph explaining the concept of TQM.

> TQM stands for Total Quality Management. This is a system which involves the whole company in the management of the quality of its services or products. For example, using the system to identify needs, agree aims and allocate responsibilities. So, TQM can be seen as a strategy to improve quality management in its broadest sense.

The explanation above can be divided into four main steps. Look at the step-by-step version in the flow chart.

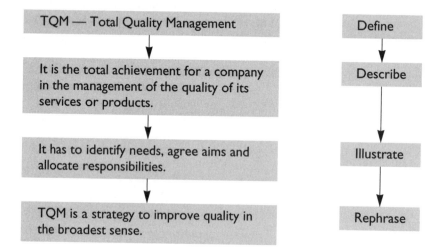

TQM — Total Quality Management → Define

It is the total achievement for a company in the management of the quality of its services or products. → Describe

It has to identify needs, agree aims and allocate responsibilities. → Illustrate

TQM is a strategy to improve quality in the broadest sense. → Rephrase

Now read the paragraph below and in the same way break down the information into steps to make a flow chart.

> Market research is the investigation of the needs and potential of a market. It involves several stages including the definition of objectives, the collection and analysis of results, and finally the interpretation and presentation of findings. For example, a company may use market research to decide on the likely demand for a product at a given price. To summarise, market research enables companies to make informed decisions about marketing strategy and its implementation.

3.2.2   Now take a concept or term related to your own work, or if you prefer, take the term *brainstorming* and explain it in the same step-by-step way – define, describe, illustrate, rephrase.

Record your own explanation then listen to your recording, checking that you included all the steps. Prepare notes and, if possible, give your explanation in class or to a partner.

Explaining visual information

Simple bold visuals can help explain concepts clearly. The graph below shows the variation in production costs during a ten-month period.

3.2.3   Look at the graph and match the phrases with the corresponding section.

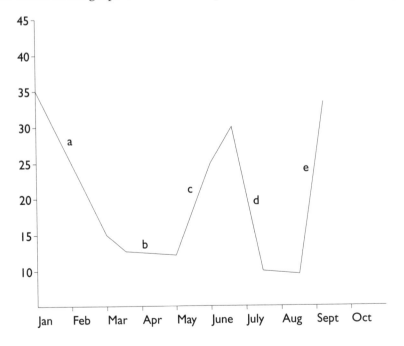

a dramatic rise	a moderate decrease
a gradual fall	a steep drop
a levelling-off	a sharp fall
a sudden increase	a stable period

3.2.4

We can describe movements on a graph or chart in two ways:

a) There was **a sudden increase** in costs **of** 10%.
b) Costs **suddenly increased by** 10%.

a) There was **a gradual fall** in costs **from** 15m **to** 12m.
b) Costs **gradually fell by** 3m.

Now complete the sentences below which refer to the graph on page 15.

1 As you can see in the graph, costs .... in the first two
   months.
2 In March, costs continued to .... but more ....
3 Costs .... 15m .... 12m during this period.
4 During the next one and a half months there was a ....
   .... of costs.
5 However, in mid May they .... 25m.
6 In June they continued to .... but more ...., ... 25m
   .... 28m.
7 In the next two months costs .... again .... 12m.
8 However, the trend changed in September when costs ....
   .... to 32m.

3.2.5

Now, using the following bar chart, make five sentences to describe the
most significant points.

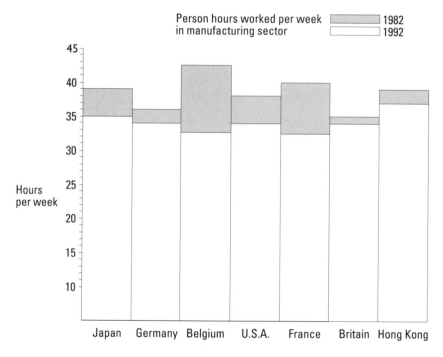

Person hours worked per week in manufacturing sector — 1982 / 1992

Hours per week

Japan Germany Belgium U.S.A. France Britain Hong Kong

Compare your sentences with the models on cassette. Practise
speaking your description of the bar chart.

3.3   Business focus – Quality management

Here is a list of words from the interview which are commonly used in a wide variety of business situations.

3.3.1   Complete the list of nouns and verbs. Use a dictionary to check any unfamiliar words.

Nouns	Verbs
....	to maximise
optimum	....
standard	....
....	to achieve
prevention	....
aim	....
success	....
failure	....
....	to manage
....	to control
calculation	....
....	to measure
....	to reduce
investment	....

Now underline the stressed (i.e. most prominent) syllables in the list of words above.

3.3.2   The sentences on the cassette contain the words listed above. Listen and practise saying them.

3.3.3   Now draw a graph related to your own work or studies and present it to the group or a partner.

Here are some ideas to help you:

- Company sales during the last 12 months
- Holiday periods throughout the year
- Your energy level during the day

Before you present your graph, study these phrases.

As you can see in the graph ...
As the graph/diagram illustrates ...
If you look at the graph ...
The vertical axis above shows ...
The horizontal axis represents/indicates ...

Phoning

4.1   Language in context

4.1.1

Most phone calls follow a certain pattern:

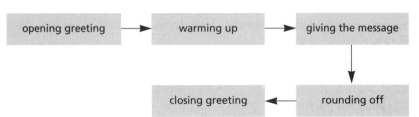

What opening greeting would you make if you a) make a call
b) receive a call?
What greetings and responses do you think the people in business would
make?

4.1.2

[cassette icon] Listen to the telephone conversation between Clive Farmer and his
interviewer, Julie Robson. Decide if the statements are **true** or **false**.

1 Clive Farmer made the phone call.
2 He is at work.
3 Julie interviewed him yesterday.

4 She left something in his office by mistake.
5 She'll pick up the file today.
6 Clive was happy to be interviewed.

4.1.3

Look at the following phrases from the telephone conversation between Clive and Julie, and match the phrases with the stages on the right.

Phrase	Stage
1 OK. Goodbye then.	
2 What can I do for you?	a) opening greeting
3 I think I left a file in your office.	b) warming up
4 Hello, Dr Farmer. This is Julie Robson.	c) giving the message
5 You remember I interviewed you?	d) rounding off
6 Thanks again for your time.	e) closing greeting
7 Would you mind putting it in the post?	
8 Don't mention it. I enjoyed it.	

4.1.4

Sit back to back with a partner and make an imaginary phone call inviting them to meet for a drink or to go to the cinema with you. Note how you follow the stages of the call.

4.2 Social language – Telephoning tactics

Study the following table of phrases and responses. Some you will need for phoning through a company switchboard.

Stage	Phrase	Response
Opening	Good morning / Hello. This is / It's ...	Good morning / Hello. Who's calling, please?
Warming up	I'd like to speak to ... Could/Can I speak to ...? How are you?	Just a minute, I'll put you through. Hold on, I'll get him/her. Nice to hear from you.
Giving the message	I'm phoning about ... Could you give X a message?	I'm sorry s/he's not in. The line's busy. Will you hold? I'll give him/her the message.
Rounding off	Thanks for your help. Fine/Great/OK. I look forward to seeing/ meeting you.	Thank you for calling. OK/Right/Fine. Me too.
Closing	Goodbye (then). Goodbye for now.	Goodbye. Bye.

4.2.1

Complete the following telephone conversations with appropriate phrases from the table.

A

Receptionist: Tudor Hotel. Good morning.
Caller: .... Mr Clayton, please?
Receptionist: ...., please?
Caller: .... Chris Jones.
Receptionist: Right, Mr Jones, ...
Caller: Thank you.

B

Mrs Thomas: Hello, 652 011.
Jack: Hello. .... Diane, please? ....
.... Jack.
Mrs Thomas: Hello, Jack. .... ?
Jack: Fine thanks, Mrs Thomas.
Mrs Thomas: I'm sorry, Diane's ....
Jack: .... a message?
Mrs Thomas: Yes, of course.
Jack: I'm .... the party this evening. What time shall I pick her up? Will you ask her to phone me?
Mrs Thomas: Right. I'll .... message.
Jack: Thanks. Bye.
Mrs Thomas: ....

Check your dialogues with the conversations on the cassette.

4.3 Role play

Practise two telephone calls with a partner. Make sure you include the different stages. In each call learner A makes the call and learner B receives the call.

Learner A turn to page 86 in the Resource Section for instructions.
Learner B turn to page 93 in the Resource Section for instructions.

Case study 1

This case study is designed to:
1 reinforce presentation skills practised in Units 1 and 3;
2 provide further practice and expand business vocabulary;
3 activate speaking skills in a business context.

Structure

This case study concerns a German sports equipment manufacturer called *Tumidas AG*. It has two parts.

Part 1 Background information: 1 General
                                  2 Market
                                  3 Finance
                                  4 Production and Distribution
                                  5 Organisation

Part 2 Problem and solutions: 1 The problem
                                  2 Possible solution A
                                    Possible solution B

Classroom management

Groups

1 Present the objectives and structure of the case study.
2 Explain that this is an opportunity to use presentation skills in context. Your role is to monitor and give feedback after the case study on their performance.

Part 1 Background information

1 **All** the learners should see the general information (1). Give them time to absorb the general information.
2 The rest of the information (2–5) should be shared out between sub-groups.
3 Each sub-group should prepare a short presentation on the information.
4 Each sub-group presents the information (using transparencies or the board).
5 The other groups can ask questions to clarify the information.
6 At the end of the activity each member of the group should have a 'total' picture of the situation.

Part 2   Problem and solutions

1 Divide into two groups. Both groups should study the problem.
2 Allocate solution A to one group, solution B to the other group.
3 Each group should use the background information they have collected and the suggested solution to make a presentation.

Pairs

Work as above except share the information between the two individuals to create an information gap.

Individuals (one-to-one)

Part 1 – The learner can study all the background information for homework, then present it to the teacher.
Part 2 – The learner can present solution A; the teacher, solution B.

Individuals working alone

Working by yourself, you should study all the information and practise presenting the visual information using a cassette recorder.

Part 1

1 General information

Check through the facts below. Make sure you have a clear picture of the development of the company.

Tumidas AG

Brief History

1922	Founded by Wolfgang Sadim. He started a small textile firm in Stuttgart called *Sadim Gmbh*.
1950	Wolfgang Sadim died. His son, Otto, took over.
1960	Started to specialise in sports clothing.
1965	Floated on German stock exchange as *Tumidas AG*.
1970	Sports equipment division started – tennis and squash rackets.
1975	Bought Zunella, Milan – an Italian clothes company.
1980	Otto Sadim retired. Brother-in-law, Horst Muden, took over.
1989	Bought Clubline – US golf club manufacturer.

Location	Registered office and headquarters in Stuttgart, Germany.
Employees	3,500
Products	Sports clothing including Zunella label. Sports equipment: tennis, squash and golf.
Turnover (94)	$347 million
Profits (94)	$42 million

2 Market

Prepare a presentation of the market information below. Transfer the
visuals onto transparency or the board for your presentation.

1   Sports clothing: world sales and competitors

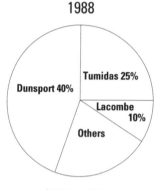

1988

$400 million

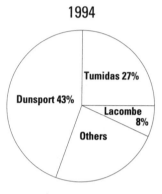

1994

$620 million

2   Sports equipment (tennis, squash and golf)

2.1 World sales   1988

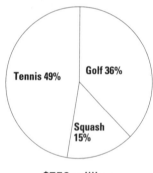

$750 million

1994

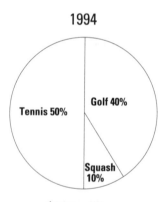

$900 million

2.2 Competitors   1988

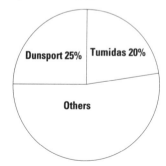

1994

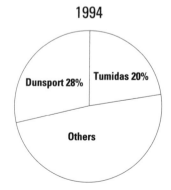

3   Finance

Prepare a presentation of the financial information below. Transfer the
visuals onto transparency or the board for your presentation.

1   Tumidas turnover 1988–1994

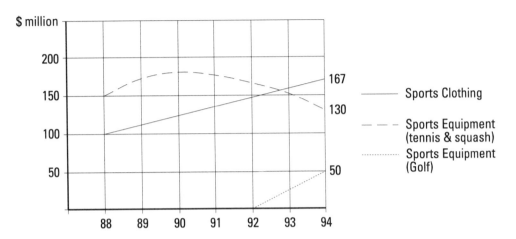

2   Tumidas profits 1988–1994

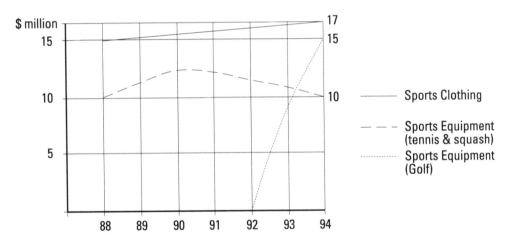

4   Production and Distribution

Prepare a presentation on the information below. Transfer the visual
information onto a transparency or the board for your presentation.

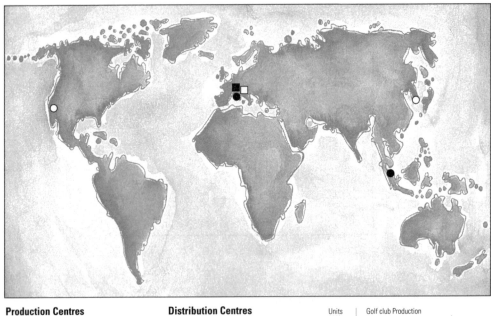

Production Centres

● Sports Clothing: Singapore
            Milan (Zurrella)

○ Sports Equipment: Korea: tennis & squash
            San Francisco: golf

Distribution Centres

■ Sports Clothing: Stuttgart
□ Sports Equipment: Munich

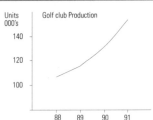

5   Organisation

Prepare a presentation on the information below. Transfer the organisation
chart onto a transparency or the board for your presentation.

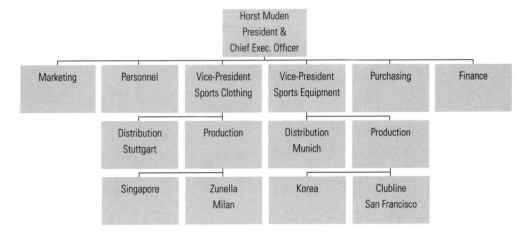

Part 2

1 The problem

Read through the problem below. Make sure you understand the situation.

> Clubline was acquired by *Tumidas AG* in 1989. It is a very successful company operating at the top end of the market. Before it was acquired, its golf clubs were sold exclusively in the US. These clubs have now been very successful in the rapidly-growing European market. This has led to a very rapid increase in production.
>
> The last consignment to arrive from the US at the Munich distribution centre was found to have a manufacturing fault. The whole consignment must be returned to San Francisco for repair.

2.1 Possible solution A

Use the background information you have collected and the suggested solution below to make a presentation.

Geoff Denny, Vice-President of Clubline, sees this as a production problem. Better production planning will avoid the problem in the future. He uses the following two charts to explain his solution.

Production output this year

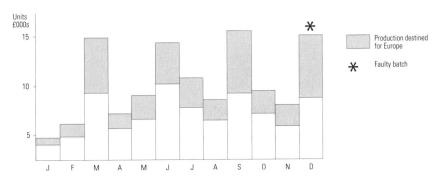

Suggested output next year

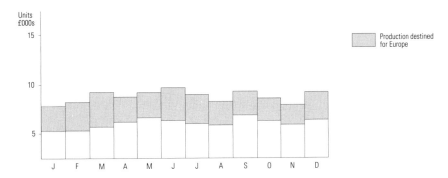

2.2   Possible solution B

Use the background information you have collected and the suggested solution below to make a presentation.

Kurt Bauer, Vice-President Equipment Division, sees this as an organisational problem. Better quality control and management will avoid this problem in the future. He uses the following two charts to explain his solution.

Clubline - present organisation

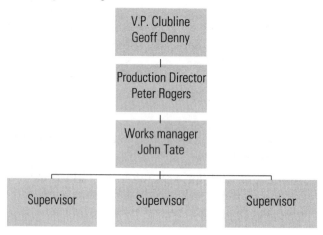

Clubline - suggested new organisation

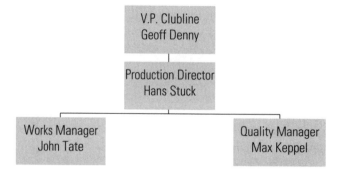

Giving and getting product information

5.1 Language in context

5.1.1 A trade fair

Have you ever attended a trade fair? If so, describe the trade fair from your experience. If not, perhaps you can describe a similar event. What sort of information do you expect to exchange at a trade fair?

5.1.2

Listen to the dialogue between a sales representative of a golf manufacturing company, Golf Pro, and a potential customer at an international golf fair. As you listen, complete the table showing the Golf Pro product ranges and prices.

Golf Pro

Product range	Price
Metal woods	.... each
Golf Pro Lady (set of 9 irons)	....
Woods (set of 3)	....
Putters	.... each
Golf Pro (set of 9 irons)	....

5.1.3

Listen again if necessary and then complete the following short report on Mr Usugi's visit to the Golf Pro stand with words and phrases from the dialogue.

International Golf Fair, Earls Court, London

12.7.

Re: Golf Pro, Japan

Golf Pro are a) .... to the golf equipment industry but are very quickly b) .... a c) .... for their products.

They are now d) .... in the production of metal woods and have a comprehensive e) .... including ladies clubs. f) .... are very competitive, their top of the range full set of irons costs £790.

All g) .... information is given in their h) .... brochures. (attached)

5.2   Language use – Giving, getting and checking information

Here are some ways of giving and getting information.

Giving
Can I help you?
Here's our latest brochure.
Prices start at ...
Perhaps you're interested in our professional range?
If you need any further help, please ask.

Getting
How much are the ...?
Does that include VAT?
Do you have a professional range?
Have you heard of our products before?
Could you give some information about the ...?
Do you think you could fax that to me?

Checking
Let me know if you want any more help, won't you?
How much did you say the ... are?
That was £39, wasn't it?
So, they're $425. Is that right?

5.2.2

Fill in the gaps in the following lines of salesperson/customer dialogue.

1 a) Can .... at all?
   b) I'm just .... thanks.
2 a) Have you .... of our .... before?
   b) No, I don't .... so.
3 a) .... are the metal woods?
   b) £85 ....
4 a) Does the price .... VAT?
   b) No, I'm afraid ....
5 a) .... tell me the price range for putters?
   b) Certainly, prices .... at about £35.
6 a) .... £35, wasn't it?
   b) Yes, ... right.

5.2.3

Rearrange the jumbled dialogue between a salesperson and a customer. Begin with the salesperson asking *Can I ...?*

Customer: I really wanted white.
Salesperson: Yes, it does.
Customer: Are there different sizes?
Salesperson: Can I help you?
Customer: The price includes delivery and installation, doesn't it?
Salesperson: There are two types of rail. The standard type here in plain metal.
Customer: Well, thank you very much.
Salesperson: Certainly, here is our brochure.
Customer: Do you supply the accessories for attaching the equipment?
Salesperson: Ah. Then the deluxe rail comes in ten different colours, including white.
Customer: Thank you.
Salesperson: Yes, the full range of accessories is described in the brochure.
Customer: Could you give me some information about rail systems for audio visual equipment?
Salesperson: The width doesn't vary but you can order any length you want.

Now check the order of the dialogue on your cassette and in pairs practise speaking it.

5.3   Business focus – Business description

5.3.**1**

Look at the following common business phrases and expressions on the left. Match them with the appropriate definition on the right.

a) top of the range   1 good enough
b) state of the art   2 the leader
c) up-to-date   3 being processed
d) out of date   4 current
e) up to scratch   5 the best quality product
f) out of production   6 no longer manufactured
g) in the pipeline   7 not current
h) first in the field   8 the very latest technology

Now listen to the phrases on the cassette and practise the rhythm, e.g.: – – – . . – – –
     TOP of the RANGE

5.4   Role play

5.4.1

For the role play information turn to the Resource Section at the back of the book.

Role A page 87
Role B page 92

5.4.2

Now prepare a similar role play, with a partner, but this time use information related to your own professional situation. Make sure you practise the different ways of giving and getting information. Record and then evaluate your dialogue.

Small talk

6.1 Language in context

6.1.1
Chatting, or small talk, in a party or group situation is difficult for many of us, especially in another language. Which topics would you choose to talk about with someone you have just met at a conference? You have already discussed work and where you both come from.

health	sport	sex	politics	current affairs
family	religion	food	books	the venue
TV/cinema	music	theatre	art	holidays

Which topics are traditionally *taboo* when talking to strangers?

6.1.2
 Listen to the conversation between the Golf Pro sales representative, Genevieve Hubert, and two sales reps from another stand. Decide if these statements are **true** or **false**.

1 It is lunchtime.
2 Genevieve offers Jane a drink.
3 Brian is a colleague of Genevieve's.
4 The bar is always very busy.
5 Genevieve is going to Scotland on holiday.
6 She is leaving the following evening.

6.2 Social language – Giving encouragement

An important part of conversation is encouraging the other speaker to continue. We do this by using a variety of expressions to give positive feedback.

fine	great	good idea
right	OK	that would be nice
sure	of course	sounds interesting
I see	really	me too

6.2.1

Complete the following dialogue with some encouraging 'small talk' expressions for Role A.

A Did you take a holiday last year?
B Yes. We went on one of those activity holidays in the Pyrenees.
A ....
B Yes, it was very good. So well-organised and not expensive.
A .... ?
B Yes. It's difficult to find a holiday to suit all the family.
A ....
B Personally, I like to get away from people.
A Mmm. ....
B But the children prefer lots of organised activity.
A ....
B We may do the same sort of thing but in Greece this year.
A ....
B I've always liked the idea of a watersports holiday.
A ....
B What about yourself? What did you do last year?

Compare your answers with the models on cassette, then in pairs practise speaking the dialogue.

6.2.2

We can also make conversations more positive by using emphasis, i.e. by using emphatic words and strong word stress. Complete this table of emphatic adjectives and adverbs and underline the stressed syllable in each word, e.g. eNORmous   eNORmously

adjective	adverb
terrific	....
....	amazingly
incredible	....
fantastic	....

Practise pronouncing the words aloud by repeating them after the cassette.

6.2.3   Look at these pairs of sentences.

The game was OK.
The game was fanTAStic.

Our trip was interesting.
Our trip was inCREdibly interesting.

The second sentence in both pairs is much more enthusiastic. Now change the words in **bold** so that the dialogue below sounds more positive. More than one answer is possible.

A We went to see that new film last night.
B Oh, what was it like?
A **Quite** funny.
B Mmm.
A Then we went to the Thai restaurant for a meal.
B Oh really, was it good?
A It was **OK.**
B Yes?
A **Quite** a friendly atmosphere. **Reasonable** service.
B What about the food?
A **So so.** Try it yourself sometime.
B Maybe. It's a bit pricey though, isn't it?
A No, actually, it's **fairly** cheap.

6.3   Role play

6.3.1   For the role play information turn to the Resource Section at the back of the book.

Role A page 89
Role B page 92

6.3.2   You and your partner were introduced a few minutes ago at a conference reception. You have already talked about where you are from, the weather and you know his/her job. Continue the conversation on topics such as:

- pros and cons of the conference venue
- previous conferences
- opinion of the speaker, etc.

Give positive feedback to the other speaker and use emphatic words to show enthusiasm where possible.

Unit 7

Dealing with visitors

7.1   Language in context

7.1.1   Visiting a factory

1 What are the possible functions of the buildings in the photograph?
2 Why do business people sometimes visit factories?
3 What sort of questions may a prospective customer ask?

7.1.2

▭ Listen to the conversation and complete the description of the company.

Flexipak is a leading company in Italy in the production of flexible a) .... Our production unit covers b) .... square metres. c) .... of this area is reserved for raw materials and finished products while the remaining two thirds is the factory building itself. Flexipak has developed rapidly in the last few years and we export d) .... of total production. Turnover last year reached e) .... Our packaging is used all over the world to pack a variety of products, particularly foodstuffs such as biscuits, coffee and chewing gum and also f) .... such as aspirin. Since it was established in g) .... , our company has developed a h) .... stock control system in the warehouse, i) .... sorting and the most j) .... checking instruments in the quality control lab.

7.1.3   Now listen again and pick out the expressions used to:

1 welcome visitors

....

....

2 offer to show someone round

....

3 point out different features

....

....

4 respond to the host

....

....

....

7.2   Language use

7.2.1   Study the sentences below and in particular notice the verb forms we use to:

a) **Explain functions and processes**
One third of this area **is for** storage of raw materials.
The lab **is where** we test and evaluate our products.
The other third **is used for** the production process itself.

b) **Give facts**
We **export** about 40% of total production.
The warehouse is highly **automated.**
We **use** bar codes.
The company **was established** in 1971.
The factory **was completed** in 1981.

c) **Ask for information**
Could you give me some information about the company?
Could you tell me a little about the staff?

d) **Ask for clarification**
What exactly do you mean by **multi-layer packaging?**
I'm not very clear **what laminates are.**

7.2.2

The flow chart below shows the processing of an order. Use the flow chart to describe the order process to a partner.

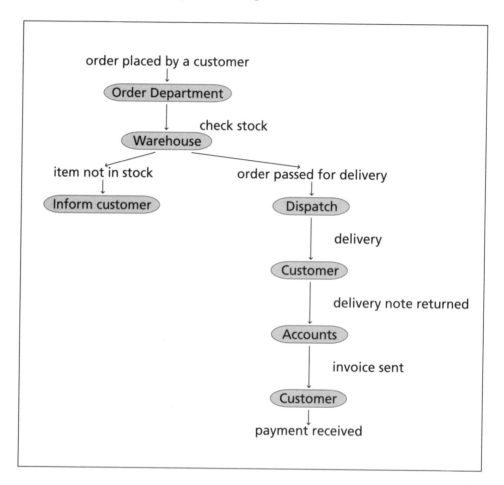

7.2.3

Practise explaining a function or process related to your work to a partner. Your partner must ask for explanations or clarification if something is not clear. When you have finished, your partner must summarise what s/he has understood of your explanation.

7.3   Business focus

7.3.**1**   Using nouns in groups

In technical descriptions we often use nouns and adjectives in groups, e.g. a code in the form of bars which is read electronically = electronic bar code.

Now complete the list.

1 Packaging which has multiple layers.   ....
2 A system for controlling stock using a computer.   ....
3 A laboratory which controls the quality of products.   ....
4 Instruments which are used for checking and are up-to-date.   ....
5 Methods of production which are new.   ....
6 A system of sorting which is automated.   ....

Now listen to the groups of words on the cassette and practise the pronunciation.

7.4   Role play

7.4.**1**

In pairs, prepare and act out a dialogue between two business people. Turn to the Resource Section at the back of the book for the role play information: Role A – Personnel Manager of Foramor Tools – see page 88; Role B – the visitor – see page 86.

7.4.**2**

Now draw a plan of your own company building. With a partner simulate a tour of the building pointing out places and explaining functions to a visitor.

Unit 8

Offering help and Invitations

8.1   Language in context

8.1.1   Places to eat

Where would you take a business visitor to eat in your home town or city? What food might you suggest as a starter, main course and dessert?

8.1.2

Listen to the cassette and decide if these statements are **true** or **false**.

1 Mr Williams asks Sr Balazzo to recommend something on the menu.
2 Both of them choose *pollo venezia*.
3 Sr Balazzo invites Mr Williams to dinner the next evening.
4 Sr Balazzo offers to collect Mr Williams at eight o'clock.
5 Mr Williams has an appointment at 2.30.

8.1.3   Listen to the lunch conversation again and complete these sentences from the dialogue.

1 .... recommend something?
2 .... have *pollo venezia*.
3 I .... your meal.
4 .... from your hotel at eight o'clock.
5 .... to Senora Grotto's office.

8.2   Social language

A Offering help and inviting:

> **I'll** show you to his office.
> **Let me** pick you up at your hotel.
> **Would you like me to** recommend something?
> **Can I** get you a taxi?
> **Could I** invite you to dinner?

B Accepting offers and invitations:

> **That's very kind of you.**
> Thank you, **I'd like that very much.**
> Yes please, **if it's no bother/trouble.**
>   **if you don't mind.**
> **That would be** wonderful.

8.2.1   Now complete the dialogue with appropriate phrases.

A Here's the menu, Mr Clarke.
B Thank you. Goodness, it's all in Greek!
A Yes, I'm afraid so. ....
    recommend something?
B ...., thank you.
A Well, let's see. There's *dolmades*, that's vine leaves stuffed with spiced meat.
B That sounds nice.
A By the way, before I forget, ...
    .... to dinner at my home this evening, if you're free?
B ...., thank you very much.

8.2.2   Listen to the prompts on the cassette and give appropriate replies after the tone. A model response is given after each pause.

8.3   Role play

Draw up a short menu of dishes typical of your country. Then with a partner, practise a dialogue where you:

1 invite a visitor to lunch
2 recommend (and explain) something on the menu
3 invite him/her to dinner that evening (in a good restaurant in town)
4 offer transport for the evening

Take it in turns to play the two different roles. When you are satisfied with your dialogue, record and play it back reviewing the language you have practised in this unit.

'I believe I'll skip the appetizer. I ate the flowers.'

Drawing by Levin; © 1978 The New Yorker Magazine, Inc.

Case study 2

This case study is designed to:

1 reinforce question and answer techniques practised in Units 5 and 7;
2 provide further practice and expand business vocabulary;
3 activate speaking skills in a business context.

Structure

This case study concerns *Frutti SA*, a Spanish subsidiary of a UK soft drinks company, *Frutti Drinks plc*. It consists of two parts.

Part 1 Investigation of a problem	1 The problem
	2 Briefing of two teams:
	  • the consultants (A)
	  • the managers (B)
	3 Consultant/manager interviews

Part 2 Recommendations to solve the problem	1 Briefing of two teams:
	  • the consultants (A)
	  • the managers (B)
	2 A meeting to discuss recommendations

Classroom management

Groups

1 Present the objectives and structure of the case study.
2 Explain that this is an opportunity to use question and answer techniques in context. Your role is to monitor and give feedback after the case study on the learners' performance.

Part 1   Investigation

1 All members of the group should read through the description of the problem (1). Alternatively, you can present this orally.
2 Divide the group into two sub-groups (ideally two groups of 4):
   • the consultants (A)
   • the managers (B)
3 Elect a team leader (a chief consultant and a managing director).
4 Each group should study the relevant briefing information and prepare themselves for the interviews.
5 Conduct the interviews.
6 Get into the sub-groups again to share information and impressions.

Part 2   Recommendations

1 Explain that the consultants must now present their findings and recommendations to the managers.
2 The consultants should prepare for the meeting by studying the briefing notes.
3 The managers should prepare by studying the checklist.
4 Hold the meeting.

Pairs

Work as above except share the information between the two individuals to create an information gap.

Individuals

Work as above except allocate the consultants' role and managers' role between yourself and your learner(s).

Individuals working alone

Study the problem and then the consultants' briefing information (A). Prepare some questions for the managers. Then study the managers' briefing information to see what answers you would get.

Part 1

1   The problem

Frutti Drinks plc has recently rationalised its distribution system worldwide. An important part of this rationalisation is the installation of a computer system (called *Distfrut*) to handle ordering and stock control. During the last year, each subsidiary has implemented the new system.

Frutti SA, their Spanish subsidiary, has been on-line with the UK central computer for more than 6 months. However, the procedures are not being followed and the company has continued to order stock by telex every two months.

Frutti Drinks plc has decided to send a team of consultants to investigate the problem.

2   The briefings

A Consultants' briefing information

Your job is to find out why Frutti SA is not using the Distfrut computer system. You have arranged the following meetings:

1 with the Managing Director,
2 with the Distribution Manager,
3 with the Sales Manager,
4 with the Finance Manager.

For each meeting you will find a checklist below of question areas. Remember to warm up at the beginning of each meeting with some small talk. ,

Consultants' checklists for interviews

Managing Director

Background information
- number of employees
- organisation of the subsidiary
- results (turnover and profits)
- market conditions

Distfrut system
- overview of the system
- hardware installation date
- user training sessions
- on-line date
- problem: reason for non-use

Distribution Manager

Background information
- organisation of Distribution Department
- distribution network
- other comments

Distfrut system
- terminals installed when?
- training carried out
- on-line date
- problem: reason for non-use

Sales Manager

Background information
- organisation of the Sales Department
- sales network
- other comments

Distfrut system
- terminals installed when?
- training carried out
- on-line date
- problem: reason for non-use

Finance Manager

Background information
- organisation and responsibilities
- financing stock

Distfrut system
- terminals installed when?
- training carried out
- on-line date
- problem: reason for non-use

B Managers' briefing information

Managing Director – data sheet

Your job is to answer any questions the consultant may have. Read through the information below before your interview. Remember to start each interview with some small talk.

Organisation

Other staff 3 secretaries
Total staff 31

Results – last year's sales

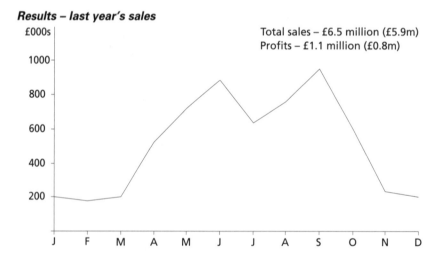

Market

Very competitive but expanding, price and delivery very important.

Distfrut system

- terminals installed March last year
- training sessions April and May
- on-line June 1st
- problem: not used because Sales Manager is not interested in computers

Distribution Manager – data sheet

Your job is to answer any questions the consultant may have. Read through the information below before your interview. Remember to start each meeting with some small talk.

Organisation

Distribution network

NOTE: orders from wholesalers not regular.

Distfrut system

- terminals installed March last year
- training good
- on-line beginning of June
- problem: worked for 2 months; now not used because there is no input from the Sales Department

Sales Manager – data sheet

Your job is to answer any questions the consultant may have. Read through the information below before your interview. Remember to start each meeting with some small talk.

Organisation

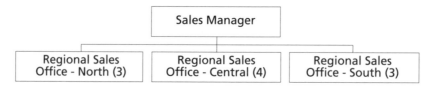

Sales network

Notes:
- very competitive market for price and delivery
- wholesalers – very difficult to get them to make regular orders
- sales management – a lot of travel, no time for administration

Distfrut system

- terminals installed in March last year
- training offered but no time
- on-line June 1st
- problem: impossible to input monthly sales forecasts because:
  - i) wholesalers work on a 2-monthly basis
  - ii) no time – need an assistant
  - iii) no training in use of the computer.

Finance Manager – data sheet

Your job is to answer any questions the consultant may have. Read through the information below before your interview. Remember to start each meeting with some small talk.

Organisation

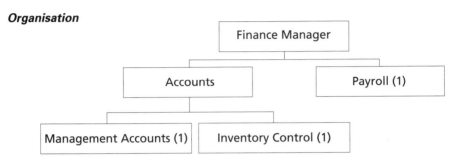

000s units   Level of stock (last year)

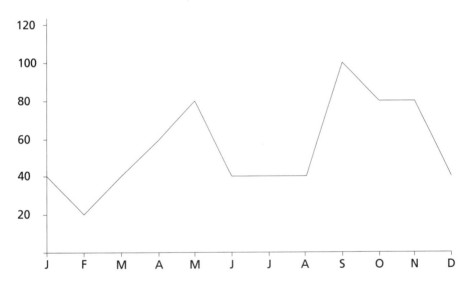

Notes: Distfrut system operation for 2 months – June and July.
         Rest of the year – inventories high and unpredictable.

Distfrut system

- terminals installed in March last year
- training carried out – yes, good
- on-line date June 1st
- problem: system only ran for 2 months (see graph); since then, no input from the Sales Department.

3 The interviews

The consultants now conduct separate interviews with:
1 The Managing Director
2 The Distribution Manager
3 The Sales Manager
4 The Finance Manager

Part 2

1 The briefings

Your task is now to take part in a meeting between the managers and the consultants. The objectives of this meeting are for the consultants to:
1) report their findings to the managers
2) make recommendations to the managers.

To help you prepare for the meeting there are some briefing notes below:
A Briefing notes for the consultants
B Checklist for the Managing Director

A Briefing notes for the consultants

Use the information you gathered to answer the Managing Director's questions. Then make recommendations to solve the problem. Here are some suggestions:
• reprogram the system to order on a two-monthly basis
• recruit an assistant for the Sales Manager
• replace the Sales Manager
• other suggestions?

B Checklist for the Managing Director

Check that the consultant/s have gathered all the information they need. Use the following checklist to go through the information:
• overview of the subsidiary?
• problems with distribution?
• problems with finance?
• problems with sales?
Then ask the consultant/s for their recommendations.

2 The meeting

Now hold the meeting to discuss the recommendations.

Unit 9

Meetings between colleagues

9.1   Language in context

Consider the questions below and discuss your responses with colleagues.

How often do you have internal meetings at work:
• between colleagues in the same office?
• between different offices or subsidiaries?
Who attends them?
What are the meetings about?
How do companies (or how does your company) usually communicate internally?
Are these ways efficient?
Could they be improved?

9.1.2

⬜ An international bank with its headquarters in Switzerland and several subsidiaries in Europe and Asia is worried about its internal communications. A working party has produced a report on the situation. Listen to the meeting at which the Working Party chairman discusses the report with Personnel Assistants from three other branches: Madrid, Hong Kong and London. As you listen, complete the notes below.

Notes

1 number of documents actually received ....

2 types of communication included   ....

3 number of original sheets   ....

4 change in emphasis for communication ....

5 improvements suggested at meeting   ....

6 objections to wider use of fax   ....

9.1.3

During the meeting the participants use different phrases to state opinions, and to agree and disagree with them. Listen to the cassette again and complete these sentences.

1 ....

.... the number of copies included in that figure.

2 .... that company policy stressed the

importance of communications.

3 ...., Peter. .... But we must find a

balance which is practicable.

4 .... the emphasis should be moved to

face-to-face communications.

5 .... this would be expensive?

6 Excuse me, Peter, ...

7 .... it's since the wide use of fax machines

that the paper problem has got out of hand.

9.2 Language use

There are several ways in which we can group the opinions given in the meeting. Here are three of them.

Stating
I think it's vital to point out the number of copies included in that figure.
I have always understood that company policy ...
We feel that the emphasis should ...
In my view, it's since the wide use of fax ...

Agreeing
I agree, Peter. It has. But ...

Disagreeing
Don't you think this would be ...?
But excuse me, Peter. I can't agree.

9.2.1

A   Decide into which group (*stating, agreeing, disagreeing*) these expressions would fit best.

1 I couldn't agree more.
2 In my opinion it's too late.
3 Quite so.
4 I'm not at all sure.
5 I really can't agree.
6 I'd go along with that.

B   Working in pairs, complete these short dialogues. Take it in turns to read the first statement and to reply according to the instructions.

1 I think the report is too short.   (*disagree strongly*)
2 In my opinion, training is essential.   (*agree*)
3 I feel we all have to work together.   (*agree strongly*)
4 The situation is absurd, in my view.   (*disagree*)
5 We have too few secretaries.   (*disagree, state the opposite opinion*)
6 It's too late to change things.   (*agree*)

9.2.**2** How often? How much? How many?

Look at how we reply to the following questions using *how often? how much?* and *how many?*

How often do you write to him?	– Every week.
How often do you get this magazine?	– Four times a year.
How often does she come to see you?	– Every other week.
How many sheets do you receive?	– 2,560 a month.
How much is photocopying?	– 5 pence a sheet.
How much is advertising space?	– $750 an A4 page.
How much tax do you pay on alcohol?	– £1.50 per bottle.

To show how frequently a thing happens, or to combine price with a type of article, use *a, an* or *per* (the last one is a little more precise).

Say and write down the sentences which give the following information as in the example.

Send mailshot/March and September – *We send a mailshot twice a year.*

1 publish newsletter/April, September, December
2 phone New York/noon, 3.30 p.m., 6.30 p.m.
3 contact warehouse/Week 2, 4, 6, 8 etc.
4 use electronic mail/Monday, Tuesday, Wednesday etc.
5 pay for the use of the fax/50 pence for every A4 sheet
6 receive a circular/Tuesday, Thursday etc.

9.3   Business focus – Business communications

9.3.1

From this list of types of communication, select the type which goes best with each of the definitions that follow.

telex	electronic mail	telephone
questionnaire	telephone conference	circular
letter	mobile telephone	memo (or memorandum)
fax	video conference	brochure
report	survey	

1 a short note sent to a colleague in the same company, giving routine information.
2 a message sent from one computer to another, where it can be read immediately, or stored for later.
3 a printed, factual description of specific information, often of several pages.
4 a meeting held between people who can hear each other but not see each other.
5 a glossy coloured document, often short, giving details of a product or service.

9.3.2

Complete the following sentences with a suitable means of communication.

1 These plans of the building need to be in Toulouse today. Could you please send them by .... ?
2 In order to collect individual information from all our employees we sent out a .... to each one.
3 Instead of holding a meeting which involved extensive travelling, the European managers saw and talked to each other by means of a ....
4 You could send a telex advising of your time of arrival, but as there is plenty of time, it will be cheaper to send a ....
5 I have carried out a .... of all our agents, and here are the results.
6 Please send this short .... to all departments, reminding them of the Managing Director's visit.

9.4   Meetings role play

You are going to participate in a short meeting about the market for your company's chemical products. Divide into groups of four and choose one role: A, B, C or D. Role play instructions are in the Resource Section.

Role A page 89
Role B page 91
Role C page 93
Role D page 95

"Here's the story, gentlemen. Sometime last night, an eleven-year-old kid in Akron, Ohio, got into our computer and transferred all our assets to a bank in Zürich."

Drawing by Stevenson; © 1983 The New Yorker Magazine, Inc.

Arranging to meet

10.1 Language in context

10.1.1 Speaking on the telephone

Below are twelve telephone terms. Use a dictionary, if necessary, to define each term. Compare your definitions in your group and where possible, give examples to describe them.

international code	directory enquiries
country code	call collect
area code	call tariff
STD	personal call
operator call	emergencies
crossed line	bad line

10.1.2   Mariluz Rivera is going to visit England for a Personnel Management conference. She phones her friend and colleague, Andrea Thompson, to see if they can meet socially. Listen to the recording of their conversation, and complete the information on the data sheet below.

```
      Mariluz Rivera called from   1  ..............................
              to Andrea Thompson in   2  ..............................
   Personnel Mgt. Conference is in   3  ..............................
                          Dates      4  ..............................
   Participant from London office is  5  ..............................
   The women decide to meet in (place) 6  ..............................
                    on (date)        7  ..............................
                    at (time)        8  ..............................
                  for (meal)         9  ..............................
```

10.2   Social language

10.2.1   **Suggesting and agreeing times and places**

Look at these examples from the conversation.

- How about meeting in London?
- What about after the conference?
- Would you like to meet for lunch?
- I suggest that I come and meet you at the bank.
- Let's say 12.30.
- Yes, that's possible.
- Good idea.
- Great!

Working with a partner, use the following prompts to make suggestions and replies.

Example: A lunch/today?
                    B no good/tomorrow?
                    A How about meeting for lunch today?
                    B Today's no good. What about tomorrow?

1 A game of tennis/Saturday?
  B no good/Sunday?
2 A a restaurant/Friday evening?
  B yes/the new Mexican place?
3 A a football match/at the weekend?
  B yes/tickets for the game on Saturday
4 A cinema/tonight?
  B no good/tomorrow?
5 A a drink/after work?
  B ok/6.30

10.2.2   Listen to the phone conversation again, and note how the time prepositions are used.

in April	a period of time
on the 19th **on** Friday **on** the 23rd	a day or date
at 12.30	a point in time

Remember the common exceptions to this rule:

at the week-end, **at** Christmas, etc.
and
yesterday/today/tomorrow
this morning, this afternoon, this evening ⎫ no preposition used
tonight, last night ⎭

Now complete these sentences, using the right prepositions, where necessary.

1 I'll meet you (*tomorrow/6 p.m.*).
2 We'll see you (*week-end*) or (*Monday*).
3 She'll talk to them (*tonight*).
4 He skis (*winter*) and plays tennis (*summer*).
5 The castle was built (*the 18th century*).
6 The next world conference is (*1995*).
7 He rang me (*last night/midnight*).
8 We'll visit the family (*Christmas*).
9 Let's meet (*next Wednesday/the evening*).
10 Let's meet (*tomorrow/9 o'clock*).
11 Sorry she's not available (*the moment*), but she'll be back (*2 o'clock*).
12 The child was born (*Wednesday 8th May/11.30/the morning*).

10.2.3 Write out the following jumbled conversation in the correct order.

A Fine. What time were you thinking of?

B Hello, David, this is Elisabeth Hollins from Conway Communications.

B Fine thanks, how about you?

B Me too. Bye, David.

B Yes, that's fine by me. Shall we meet in your office or mine?

A David Unwin speaking.

A Is 9 o'clock OK for you?

B Fine, David. So that's next Monday, the 8th, in your office?

B Yes, that's fine. What time suits you best?

A Not too bad. Very busy, as usual.

A That's right. I look forward to seeing you then, Elisabeth.

A Hello, Elisabeth, how are you?

A Bye, Elisabeth. Thanks for ringing.

A I'm afraid that's not too good for me; I have a meeting. Does Monday the 8th suit you?

A Let's make it my place; then you can talk to my people about your ideas.

B How about next Wednesday, the 10th?

B Look, David, I'm ringing to see if we can arrange a time for a meeting to discuss your new publicity campaign.

Check your dialogue with the key and on the cassette, and practise it with a partner.

10.3 Role play

For the role play information turn to the Resource Section at the back of the book.

Role A page 96
Role B page 95

Prepare what you are going to say (Role A or Role B). Then sit back to back with a partner to simulate the phone call. A rings B. Try and keep the conversation going.

Record the conversation if possible, then play it back and give feedback on each other's performance.

Unit 11

Informal negotiations

11.1   Language in context

11.1.1

When a sales representative and a customer are negotiating a deal, price is one of the most important factors. However, there are often several other important considerations to discuss before they arrive at 'the bottom line'. Can you list at least five of these? Compare your lists in groups and then compare your conclusions with those in the key.

11.1.2

Bill Klyne, a sales representative for a small company manufacturing credit cards, is talking to Ed Murray, Purchasing Manager of a national bank, about the bank's order for next year. As you listen to the cassette, complete Bill's notes on the meeting.

Meeting with Ed Murray, Baltimore City Bank

Last year's price		(1)...................	
Next year:		number	price
	original offer	700,000	(2)...................
	next offer	(3)...................	18 cents
	final offer	(4)...................	(2)...................
Delivery time promised		(5)...................	
Complaint mentioned		(6)...................	
My suggestion		(7)...................	

11.1.3

Look at the following list of phrases (1–6) used for introducing topics. Match each introductory phrase with the best comment from the second list (a–f).

1 I would like to mention a couple of things here, Bill ...
2 And what about the question of ...
3 I'd like to mention ...
4 Look, what I wanted to talk to you about was ...
5 I tell you what, ...
6 I've got to tell you straight, ...

a) ... this problem of delivery.
b) ... the quality and the packaging of the product.
c) ... this just isn't good enough.
d) ... why not try something different?
e) ... that we weren't too happy with delivery times.
f) ... rising prices.

Check your sentences with those on the cassette and practise speaking them.

11.2 Language use

11.2.1 Making conditions

Look at these examples of sentences which refer to the future.

a) I can keep the price at the same level if you can increase the number of cards.
b) If you increase the price, we'll decrease the order.
c) If prices fall, I will let you know.

In sentences of this type which refer to the future, the combination of tenses can be *either* **If + present + present** (example (a)) *or* **If + present + future** (examples (b) and (c))

Make sentences with the information below, as in the following example.

Example: you/ make a good offer/ I/ accept
If you make a good offer, I'll accept.

1 the parts/ arrive on time/ production/ start immediately
2 you/ call tomorrow/ I/ have time to talk
3 you/ increase the order/ I/ lower the price
4 we/ not leave soon/ we/ arrive too late
5 we/ take quality control seriously/ standards/ improve
6 they/ promise to deliver on time/ we/ can be sure they will
7 you/ tell me your arrival time/ I/ meet you at the airport

11.2.**2**   Stalling

In negotiations you sometimes have to say things which are not very easy. In these cases you may need to take a little time to think about the next step. Look at the language in these extracts from Ed and Bill's negotiation.

Well, maybe, er ... it really depends on the price.
Well, I don't know, Bill ... .
Wait a minute, Bill.
I'll think about that, Bill.
I'll look into that, Ed.
Can I get back to you on that one?

Practise with a partner. One person reads the sentences below, the other replies according to the instructions in brackets, using the phrases above or something similar.

1 Can you tell me what happened to the latest delivery? (*look into*)
2 We need to take a decision straight away. (*wait*)
3 Can you come to the course in June? (*think*)
4 How many components will you need next month? (*don't know*)
5 Would you like to order more next year? (*depends on price*)
6 What is your attitude to using sub-contractors? (*can't say now*)

Listen to the model answers on the cassette.

11.3   Business focus – Materials management and logistics

The columns below show the different activities of a typical large company.

Things	People/Place	Process	Verb
parts	sub-contractor		
raw materials	supplier	supply	to supply
components	purchaser	purchasing/	to purchase/ buy
		production	to produce
products/goods	factory/plant	manufacture	to manufacture
	store	storage	to store
	warehouse	distribution	to distribute
	wholesaler	delivery	to deliver
	retailer	sales	to sell
	customer		

11.3.1

Identify these processes or people.

1 The turning of materials into finished products.
2 The person who sells to the customer.
3 A manufacturer who sells a product or part to another manufacturer.
4 The process of making sure the customer receives the product.
5 A person responsible for buying materials.
6 The place where goods are manufactured.

11.3.2 Complete the sentences with a word or words from the list which follows.

1 Goods .... in the factory.

2 The purchaser .... raw materials or components from the suppliers.

3 Products .... in the factory store or in the warehouse.

4 The retailer .... products to the customer.

5 Products .... nationally by rail or by road.

6 A sub-contractor .... products to another supplier.

7 Heavy products .... to customers' homes by van or truck.

buys	are manufactured
sells	are stored/kept
supplies	are distributed
	are delivered

11.4   Negotiation role play

An electronics manufacturer of printed circuit boards (pcbs) has problems with a customer. Work in pairs or as two teams. Hold a short meeting in which all the points in each role description are discussed. Use the information given but stall when necessary. For information on the role play turn to the Resource Section at the back of the book.

Role A page 93
Role B page 87

Unit 12

Developing a conversation

12.1   Language in context

12.1.1   Social situations in business are very important in building up confidence between individuals and groups. Getting to know your client often leads to good business.

The list of questions below is used to get information from people. Put them in a more logical order, then use them to quiz your partner. Collect as much information as you can in a very short time – about one minute.

1   When did you start your present job?
2   Where do you live now?
3   What do you do?
4   Do you have a family?
5   What do you do in your spare time?
6   Are you married?
7   Where do you come from?

12.1.2

Ed Murray, Purchasing Manager for Baltimore City Bank, visits credit card manufacturer, Bill Klyne, in Washington. Over lunch they find out a little more about each other. Listen to the conversation, then answer the questions about the two men.

1 When did Ed first join the bank?
2 What department was he in then?
3 Where do the two men come from?
4 Does Bill have a family?
5 Is Ed married?
6 Does he have children?
7 What is Ed's main hobby?
8 What is happening in Baltimore next weekend?
9 Why can't Bill join Ed?

12.2 Social language – keeping the conversation going

12.2.1

Several tenses are used when people discuss their past, their present and their future. Look at these sentences from the recorded conversation.

I'm really glad you **could** make this trip. (*Present and Past simple*)
How long **have you been** with the bank? (*Present perfect*)
I **joined** about eight years ago. (*Past simple*)
We're having a sort of tournament in Baltimore next weekend. (*Present continuous with future meaning*)

Listen to the conversation again, then complete these sentences.

1 I .... a meeting in town ....

2 Purchasing ....

3 Richmond, Virginia's ....

4 We .... just .... town.

5 They .... with .... mother.

6 I .... to purchasing ....

7 I .... before plastic cards.

8 I .... Philadelphia.

9 I .... here ....

10 My wife and I .... a .... to Colorado.

11 .... in the plastic revolution

business?

12 We'll .... through the trees.

12.3   **Role play**

12.3.**1**

Working in pairs, use the roles in the Resource Section to hold a conversation for a minute or more. Introduce yourself first of all and then find out information about your partner.

Role A page 94
Role B page 96

12.3.**2**

Now find a partner you don't know very well, and work together to find out as much as you can about each other – past, present and future. Record your conversation and, on playback, check your language with the sentences in 12.1.1 and 12.1.2.

Chairing a meeting

13.1 Language in context

13.1.1

A chairperson's first duty is to start the meeting with a few words to establish the tone or state the purpose of the meeting. Try and add to the list of Chair functions below. Compare and discuss your list in your group.

The chairperson's role is to:

- start the meeting

- establish the tone

- make sure any decisions are noted (minuted)

- ....

- ....

- ....

- ....

13.1.2   Listen to this management meeting called to discuss the problem of *culture shock* caused by the takeover of a Spanish company by an American company. The chairman is Sr González, the President of Duo S.A. Spain. John Banks represents the American company, Delco. The other participants are Maggie Seabrook and Teresa Navarro. As you listen to the cassette, note whether the information below is **true** or **false**.

   1   Both companies feel that Duo has no financial control.
   2   Everyone agrees to a working party on financial management.
   3   This suggestion is minuted for action.
   4   Production planning is the next item on the agenda.
   5   The Production Manager of Duo explains the position.
   6   Teresa Navarro speaks for Duo's Human Resources Manager.

13.1.3   The actions of the Chairman are summarised below in seven points. Put them in the correct order.

   1   He invites Mr Banks to speak.
   2   He calls for a decision to be minuted.
   3   He asks for comment on Item 3.
   4   He calls the meeting to order.
   5   He asks someone to introduce the second item on the agenda.
   6   He establishes the tone.
   7   He moves on to the next item.

13.2   Language use – the chairperson's role

The chairman, Sr González, plays the important role of guiding the discussion.

Starting the meeting
So, perhaps we could call our meeting to order.
Perhaps I could start by asking Mr Banks for a few words?
Right, may we move on to the agenda then, please?

Establishing the tone
Before we begin, I should like to say that I hope the meeting will be constructive and have a positive outcome.

Bringing people in
Teresa, could you please start for us?

Opening up the discussion
Who would like to start with a comment on this?

Controlling discussion
Who agrees with ...?
We'll note this in a minute and move on ...
Does anyone object if we leave this for now and move on to ...?

Summarising
This seems a sensible and constructive suggestion.

Now find phrases like those above for dealing with these situations.

1 You would like comments on the new training plan.
2 The discussion on the new toilets has gone on for nearly an hour.
3 You'd like to change from discussing last year's figures to looking at this year's.
4 You hope for a friendly, short meeting.
5 You'd like Elizabeth to say something about our information policy.
6 Everybody is talking to each other just before the budget meeting.
7 You feel that everybody agrees that something must be done immediately.

Check your phrases with the models on the cassette. Practise speaking them.

13.3   Business focus – People and work

13.3.1

Match the words and phrases from the left-hand columns with the closest equivalent from the right-hand columns.

1 frightened	a) concerned
2 sick	b) sad
3 worried	c) spirit
4 upset	d) scared
5 morale	e) ill
6 constructive	f) finding fault
7 a radical change	g) a way of looking at things
8 attitude	h) a different approach
9 to collaborate	i) helpful, positive
10 criticism	j) to work closely together

13.3.2   Look at the following list of skills and attitudes. Write them out in order of importance. Then compare your result with a colleague's and discuss any differences.

leadership	teamwork
dealing with change	personal development
dealing with stress	communication skills
decision-making	time management
flexibility	physical fitness
dealing with difficult situations	

13.4   Meetings role play

In groups of five or six, hold a number of short meetings on the topics below, and on other topics chosen by yourselves. Take it in turns to be the chairperson, whose job it is to:

- start the discussion
- bring people in
- keep the discussion going
- control people (if necessary)
- move from point to point
- finish the discussion

Give the chairperson plenty of opportunity to exercise the role. Don't make his/her job too easy!

Meetings topics
a) Working with people from different cultures
- who has experience of this?
- are cultures really very different?
- are some more different than others?
- are some nationalities worse than others at dealing with other cultures?
- do people realise the differences? If not, how can they be made aware?
- is it necessary to change attitudes? How?

b) The problems of working in a large company
- what is large?
- are large companies impersonal?
- the benefits: organisational, salary ...?
- bureaucracy
- impersonality
- what is the ideal size of a company?

c) The usefulness of training
- types of training
- quality of training
- who benefits?
- how can you know how good it is?
- the cost and who pays it
- when? Own time or company time?
- is it cost effective?

Unit 14

Talking about people and places

14.1 Language in context

14.1.1 What is special about the town or region you live in? What would particularly interest a visitor? Make a list of twelve points – some positive, some negative – that would give visitors a good picture of your part of the world. Compare lists in your group.

14.1.2

Maggie Seabrook and Rafael González are business colleagues. They are having lunch together on Maggie's last day of her business trip to Madrid. As you listen to the conversation, label the pictures below with the Spanish sights and features which Maggie mentions.

14.1.3

Listen again and complete the questions Rafael González asks in order to guide the conversation.

1 Is this your .... ?

2 Do you think .... ?

3 Have you had the opportunity .... ?

4 And what about .... ?

5 What other .... ?

6 Did you visit any .... ?

14.2   Social language

When asking and talking about places and people, use this checklist.

1   *First visit*
Is this your first visit?   Yes, it's my first time.
Have you been to ... before?   Yes, I came 3 years ago.

2   *Impressions*
What do you think of ...?   (I think) it's really nice.
Do you like ...?   Yes, it's wonderful.
How do you like the weather?   It's a bit cold, but nice.
How do you find the people?   Really nice, and very friendly.

3   *Experiences*
What have you seen so far?   Not much yet.
                                                     I've just walked round the centre.
Have you been to the museum?   Yes, it's a fascinating place.

4   *Likes/dislikes/preferences*
What do you like best?   I don't know really.
                                                     I think I prefer the cathedral.
Anything you don't like?   I'm not too keen on the traffic.

5   *Food and wine*
How do you like the food?   It's very different.
                                                     I really enjoy the food – it's very
                                                     tasty.

6   *Plans*
What do you plan to do while   I'd like to walk around the town, do
you're here?   some shopping, see the old buildings.
Will you come back?   Yes, I'd love to. I'd like to come with
                                                     my family, on holiday.

14.2.1   Match the answers in the second column with the questions in the first.

1 What do you think of York?	a) No, it's my first visit.
2 How do you find the people?	b) I love the old streets.
3 Have you been here before?	c) Yes, I have, it's wonderful.
4 Have you visited the Minster?	d) It's a lovely place.
5 What do you like best?	e) I'd like to see the country.
6 What do you think of the	f) They're OK – a bit
restaurants?	traditional.
7 What are your plans?	g) They're very friendly.

The answers are on the cassette. Listen and then practise the dialogue with a partner.

14.3 Role play

14.3.**1**

Work in pairs. One partner plays role A, the other role B. If any information is missing, you may invent it.

Role A turn to page 97 in the Resource Section.
Role B turn to page 91 in the Resource Section.

14.3.**2**

Continue with the same partner, and in the same role, A or B. If any information is missing, you may invent it.

Role A turn to page 89 in the Resource Section.
Role B turn to page 94 in the Resource Section.

14.3.**3**

Now do a similar exercise to the one in 14.3.2 – but this time for real! Look at the list of points you made in 14.1, then ask each other's impression of your town or region. Take it in turns to be the host who asks questions and the visitor who answers them. Record your dialogues and if necessary check your language with the checklist in 14.2.

Case study 3

Objectives

This case study is designed to:
1 reinforce meeting skills practised in Units 9, 11 and 13*;
2 provide further practice and expand business vocabulary;
3 activate speaking skills in a business context.

* The case study has been designed so that the interaction will include elements typical of both internal and external meetings.

Structure

The case study concerns an American multinational chemicals company called *Lexchem Inc.* Five years ago, it acquired a Japanese pharmaceutical company called *Fumisan*. The aim of this acquisition was to establish Lexchem in Japan – a market which they had found impossible to penetrate. Lexchem headquarters have decided to establish a stronger global corporate identity – this is particularly important in Japan. The case study involves a meeting between three parties:

A **Headquarters** marketing and advertising managers;
B **Subsidiary** (Fumisan) marketing and advertising managers;
C **Chairperson** – president of the company.

It consists of two parts:

Part 1: Preparation: 1 Background information for all participants
                           2 Specialist briefing information for:
                             A **Headquarters**
                             B **Subsidiary**
                             C **Chairperson**
                           3 Sub-group meetings
Part 2: The meeting

Classroom management

Groups
1 Present the objectives and structure of the case study.
2 Explain that this is an opportunity to use meeting skills in context. Your role is to monitor and give feedback after the case study on their performance.

Part 1   Preparation

1 Divide the group into three sub-groups:
  A **Headquarters staff** (ideally 3 members)
  B **Subsidiary staff** (ideally 3 members)
  C **Chairperson** (ideally 1)

The number of participants is flexible, as long as the two major roles (headquarters and subsidiary) are covered.

2 Everybody should now receive the background information. Give them time to absorb this information.

3 They should then prepare for the meeting by reading through the specialist information. The teacher can allocate roles within the sub-groups or let the sub-group decide themselves. The specific roles are:

A **Headquarters:**
  – corporate marketing manager
  – advertising manager
  – market research assistant

B **Subsidiary:**
  – managing director
  – marketing manager
  – advertising manager

C **Chairperson**

4 Each participant should then explain/present the information to the rest of the sub-group. The Chairperson should come round to the two sub-groups and brief them on the purpose of the meeting and the agenda.

5 The sub-groups should prepare their position and arguments for the meeting.

Part 2   The meeting

The teacher (through the chairperson) should make sure the following points are borne in mind.
  1 Time is limited (90 minutes?).
  2 The meeting should try to come to a decision.
  3 It is important to maintain a positive atmosphere.

Pairs

Work as above except share the information between the two individuals to create an information gap.

Individuals

Work as above except allocate the headquarter's role and subsidiary role between yourself and your learner.

Individuals working alone

Study the background information and then the headquarter's briefing information (A). Prepare your arguments. Then study the subsidiary briefing information (B) to see what response you would get to your ideas.

Part 1

1   Background information *(to be shared by all participants)*

Lexchem

Brief history		
	1948	Founded by D. Myers Junior (pharmacist)
	1958	Merger with Lexington Chemicals, became Lexchem Inc.
	1962	Acquisition of Braniff Pharmaceuticals (US)
	1968	Acquisition of Brown Health products (UK)
	1975	Launch of Cardiatard
	1978	Cardiatard becomes No. 1 heart drug in the world
	1980	Explosion in Australian Lexchem plant – 20 die
	1984	New organic chemical discovered – Lexitone A
	1986	Acquisition of Fumisan (Japan)

Business Areas

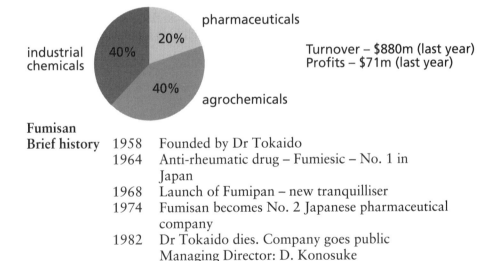

Turnover – $880m (last year)
Profits – $71m (last year)

Fumisan

Brief history		
	1958	Founded by Dr Tokaido
	1964	Anti-rheumatic drug – Fumiesic – No. 1 in Japan
	1968	Launch of Fumipan – new tranquilliser
	1974	Fumisan becomes No. 2 Japanese pharmaceutical company
	1982	Dr Tokaido dies. Company goes public Managing Director: D. Konosuke
	1986	Acquired by Lexchem. Konosuke continues as Chief Executive Officer

Business areas

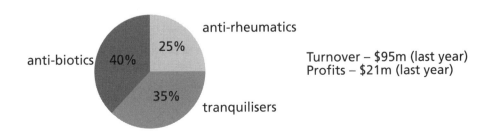

Turnover – $95m (last year)
Profits – $21m (last year)

2   Specialist briefing information

A Headquarters staff

Corporate marketing brief

Read through your brief. Explain/present the information to the rest of the group. Your chairman will give you an agenda for the meeting when you are ready. Prepare your position and arguments for the meeting.

Your objective is to give Lexchem a stronger corporate identity worldwide. At the moment, Lexchem products are only sold under the Lexchem name in the US. Elsewhere, the name is almost unknown. In other words, companies such as Brown Health UK and Fumisan Japan continue to market their own and Lexchem's products using branded names and their own companies' names. Until recently this has fitted with corporate policy which was to leave national companies to do their own business without interference from headquarters.

Now, as the market becomes more competitive, there are good reasons for imposing a corporate identity on all Lexchem's products worldwide.

Reasons for corporate identity programme:

- Lexchem name and track record are a powerful marketing tool.
- Higher profile will make advertising more effective.
- Stronger single identity will make it easier to:
    – attract new investors
    – recruit better staff
    – acquire new companies
    – give staff more opportunities for development
    – negotiate with governments and ministries worldwide.

Your specific strategy as far as Fumisan is concerned is to start using the Lexchem name on all Fumisan's and Lexchem's pharmaceutical products in Japan. Thus the name will become better known and will help the introduction of Lexchem's other products (industrial and agro-chemicals) into the Japanese market.

As part of the new corporate identity programme, you have asked the Advertising Department to come up with a corporate logo (previously only the name Lexchem has been used).

You have also asked your market research department to do some research into Fumisan's prospects over the next 10 years.

Brief your colleagues on your position and then find out what they have come up with.

Advertising brief

Read through your brief. Explain/present the information to the rest of the group. Your chairman will give you an agenda for the meeting when you are ready. Prepare your position and arguments for the meeting.

As part of a corporate identity programme, you were asked to come up with a new logo for Lexchem. You commissioned an advertising agency to put forward some ideas. Prepare your arguments for and against the agency's proposals. Discuss your ideas with your colleagues. During the meeting with Fumisan, you should be prepared to argue in favour of one of the logos.

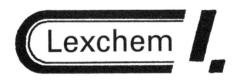

Market research brief

Read through your brief. Explain/present the information to the rest of the group. Your chairman will give you an agenda for the meeting when you are ready. Prepare your position and arguments for the meeting.

You were asked by corporate marketing to do some projections for Fumisan's growth potential over the next 10 years. You have come up with the figures in this graph.

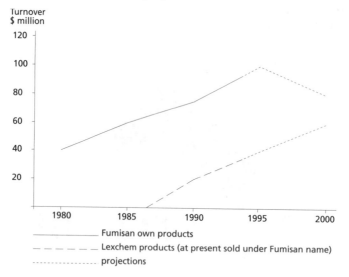

As the graph shows, your research indicates a downturn in Fumisan's own product sales in about 5 years' time, while Lexchem products continue to do well. This can be explained by the following:

- A projected downturn in Fumisan's product areas (see background information)
- An increasingly competitive market where the large multinationals start to dominate
- An increasingly interdependent world market where national product/brand names suffer

Explain your research to your colleagues and then prepare to use these arguments in the meeting with Fumisan.

B Subsidiary staff

Managing Director's brief

Read through your brief. Explain/present the information to the rest of the group. Your chairman will give you an agenda for the meeting when you are ready. Prepare your position and arguments for the meeting.

Your objective is to continue making Fumisan a successful pharmaceutical company. You are worried by news of a new corporate identity programme because of the diversification into new products (industrial and agro-chemicals) which will follow. You feel you have achieved very good results for your parent company over the last few years (you know Fumisan is Lexchem's most profitable single business operation).

You would like to continue running Fumisan as an autonomous business with only you reporting to the President of Lexchem. You have asked your Marketing Manager to prepare arguments in favour of keeping the Fumisan name and maintaining control over marketing and business strategy.

You have also asked your Advertising Manager to report on Fumisan's image and future advertising policy.

Brief your colleagues on your position and then find out what they have come up with.

Advertising Manager's brief

Read through your brief. Explain/present the information to the rest of the group. Your chairman will give you an agenda for the meeting when you are ready. Prepare your position and arguments for the meeting.

Your Managing Director has asked you to report on Fumisan's image. You have commissioned a survey which shows that:
1 Fumisan is a well-known name and associated with quality.
2 Lexchem is completely unknown.
3 Fumisan logo is also well-known and associated with quality.

You draw the following conclusion:
• future advertising strategy should continue to build on Fumisan's excellent image. Explain this to your colleagues and then prepare for your contribution to the meetings.

Marketing Manager's brief

Read through your brief. Explain/Present the information to the rest of the group. Your chairman will give you an agenda for the meeting when you are ready. Prepare your position and arguments for the meeting. You have been asked by your Managing Director to prepare arguments against the implementation of a corporate identity programme proposed by Lexchem headquarters.

You have started by projecting future business. These figures are shown in the following graph.

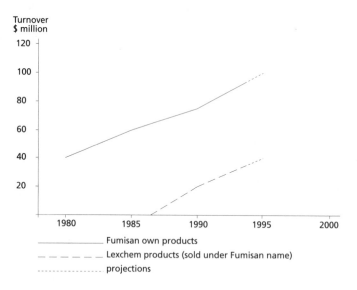

Note: You feel it is impossible to project beyond 1995 since circumstances cannot be predicted.

You draw the following conclusions:
• prospects for Fumisan and Lexchem's products are very good
• the Japanese market knows the name Fumisan and associates it with quality. There could be resistance to an American name.
• future products should continue to be marketed under the Fumisan name.
• marketing strategy should continue to be directed from Japan (knowledge of local conditions)

Explain your ideas to your colleagues and then prepare for your contribution to the meeting.

C Chairperson's brief

Read through your brief. Present the agenda for the meeting to the other two groups when they are ready. Prepare for your role as chairperson during the meeting.

You are the president of Lexchem Inc. The objective of the meeting is to decide on the implementation of a new corporate identity programme in Japan. During the meeting you must keep the following factors in mind:

1 Fumisan's successful profits record.
2 Previous policy of autonomy in the subsidiaries.
3 The need to build on Fumisan's success (introduction of new products).
4 The world market is becoming increasingly competitive.

It is your job to keep a positive atmosphere during the meeting and make sure the meeting reaches a conclusion in a given time. (maximum: 90 minutes?).
There are 3 possible outcomes:

1 full implementation of the programme
2 partial implementation
3 no implementation

Before the meeting you must distribute (or put on the board) an agenda. Look through the following proposed agenda. When the participants are ready, inform them of the agenda.

Proposed agenda

1 Lexchem's corporate identity programme.
2 Marketing strategy – worldwide and Japan.
3 Advertising strategy – worldwide and Japan.
4 Diversification in Japan.
5 Fumisan's forecast sales.
6 Lexchem's new advertising logo.

Part 2   The meeting

Resource Section

4.3   Role play

Role play 1

Learner A

You are Pat Murphy from Wellington, New Zealand. You met Leslie Jones from Dataprint when he was in New Zealand and said you would call him when you were in London. Ring Dataprint and ask to speak to him.

Role play 2

Learner A

You receive a phone call from a business friend whom you know quite well. You are going to the United States for the first two weeks in April on a training course.

7.4.1   Role play

Role B

You are visiting Foramor Tools Inc. The Personnel Manager will show you around. Ask questions about the following topics.

Number of employees
Production capacity
Turnover
Age of factory
Main export markets
Present projects

11.4   Role play

Role B the manufacturer

Your customer ordered 150 LME10 pcbs on June 16, for delivery on July 22, at $8.30 each.

Since then you have had a fire in the factory. Production has been limited and quality control made difficult.

You are doing your best to supply customers, and to replace any faulty boards.

Be apologetic, but clear and firm – and try to retain your customer.

5.4.1   Role play

Learner A

You are the representative from a ski equipment manufacturer, *Skiwhizz*. Use the information below to answer the buyer's questions.

1 Skiwhizz was established in 1981.
2 It is American-owned, but has subsidiaries in many countries in Europe and Asia.
3 Total number of employees is over 40,000.
4 Main products are downhill and cross-country ski boots and accessories.
5 Europe is your main export market, but the Japanese market is developing rapidly.
6 France is your biggest market in Europe.
7 There are agents in Germany, Switzerland and Luxemburg.
8 Skiwhizz will start manufacturing downhill skis next year.
9 And cross-country in eighteen months' time.
10 Suggest a visit at the end of the month.

7.4.1 Role play

Role A

You are the Personnel Manager of Foramor Tools Inc. Greet your visitor at reception. Show him/her to your office and make them comfortable. Offer coffee/tea. Start a general conversation. Offer to show the visitor around the offices and factory. Use the plan of the company's buildings to point out the main sections and describe their functions. Answer any questions using the information on the Data Sheet.

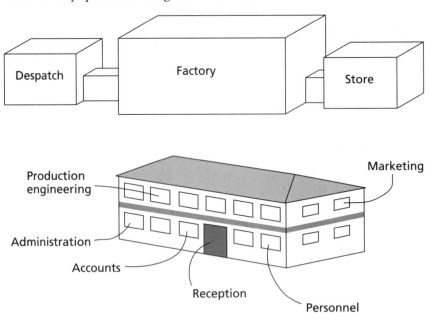

Data Sheet	Foramor Tools Inc.
No. of employees	975
	(450 admin/525 production staff)
Factory established	1985
Production capacity	1,780 units per week
Turnover (1994)	$55m
Main export markets	Scandinavia, Asia
Present project	Developing a new high-speed drilling tool (confidential)

9.4   Role play

Role A

You think the company has too many products. You think you should concentrate on your main activity – the production of domestic cleaning products. Foreign markets have always been difficult and demand is very weak at the moment.

14.3.2 Role play

Role A

You are visiting Manchester, England, where your partner lives. Use these notes to give your impressions and ideas:

- you came to Manchester three years ago, but were only travelling through.
- not as industrial as you thought. Lots of fine old buildings – but also some ugly new ones.
- the people are all very warm and friendly.
- you have been to the Museum and Art Gallery, which you liked, and been shopping in some of the large stores – rather disappointing.
- you prefer the little shops and the back streets to the large shopping arcades, and you prefer the pedestrian streets to the streets with very busy traffic.
- you had fish and chips once – not as bad as you thought. You also had a traditional pie in a local restaurant – surprisingly good.
- you would like to do some more shopping for clothes, see Manchester United play, and perhaps visit Blackpool, on the coast.

6.3.1 Role play

Role A

Tell a partner about something you did recently that you really enjoyed, e.g. a meal, a film, a sport. Stop as soon as your partner loses interest.

2.3   Role play

John Dickson
Manager
Private Business
Section

PEAT DARWIN (UK) LTD
3 Walton St. Leeds

Chris Street
Assistant Manager
Private Business
Section

PEAT DARWIN (UK) LTD
3 Walton St. Leeds

Jo Burgh
Marketing Manager

PEAT DARWIN (UK) LTD
3 Walton St. Leeds

Andrew Brunswick
Senior Partner

DATALINC
Box 283 Houston

Michele Faure
Purchasing Manager

DIGICOM
21 Bd. Joffre
Paris 16

Yugi Sakai
Manager
Bond Department
Asahi Bank
6 Shoe Lane
London
EC2M 4YD

Sven Norlin
Technical Consultant

SCANDATA
Hotorget 12
Stockholm

Carla Rocci
Assistant Director

Vetti Computers
Box 784 Milan

9.4   Role play

Role B

The home market is saturated. You should try to increase exports, particularly in South-east Asia where demand is strong. You think there are too many agents in the foreign markets. You feel a new post – Strategic Marketing Director – would help co-ordinate marketing at home and abroad.

14.3.1 Role play

Role B

You are visiting Salamanca, in Spain, and start talking to your partner, who lives there. Use these notes to give your partner your impressions and other ideas.

- this is your first visit to Salamanca (but you have been to Madrid, the capital).
- the town is much older than you thought, and really beautiful.
- the people seem very lively, and keen to speak to foreigners.
- you have only had a short walk round the centre.
- you like the old buildings, the narrow streets and the many little bars with excellent seafood. The traffic is terrible.
- the 'tapas' look very good, and you have seen some nice-looking roast meat. The wine served from large barrels also looks very attractive.
- you would like to see the University buildings, the two cathedrals (the old and new), and perhaps walk by the river. But you only have a day to do this!

6.3.1 Role play

Role B

Listen to your partner. Encourage him/her as much as possible by giving positive feedback, but do not add any information. The object is to make him/her continue speaking for as long as possible.

5.4.1 Role play

Learner B

You are a buyer for a large sports equipment store. You are meeting the representative of a ski equipment manufacturer, *Skiwhizz*. Use the list below and some of the language presented in this unit to get the necessary information.

Get information
1 young company?
2 American-owned?

Check information
3 have over 40,000 employees?

Get information
4 main products?
5 export markets in Europe only?
6 main export markets in Europe?

Check information
7 they have agents in Europe?

Get information
8 are they going to start manufacturing skis soon?
9 both downhill and cross-country?
10 a suitable date to visit their factory?

When you have practised the dialogue once with a partner, record it and then listen for:
a) appropriate question forms
b) correct language forms

9.4   Role play

Role C

The expansion from domestic cleaning products into more general production has been successful. The home market should be consolidated. Maybe you should try to buy a company that produces cleaning machinery.

4.3   Role play

Role play 1

Learner B
You are Leslie Jones' assistant. He is out for the day visiting a branch office. Ask for the caller's name and phone number and offer to ask Mr Jones to call back.

Role play 2

Learner B
You ring a business friend whom you know well and invite him/her to be guest speaker at your Communications Seminar on 12 April.

11.4   Role play

Role A the customer

June 16:	150 LME10 pcbs ordered price: $8.30 each
July 22:	90 pcbs received
August 1:	35 pcbs received
August 3:	invoice for 150 pcbs received price: $9.50 each
Complaint:	28 boards faulty, returned to the manufacturer

14.3.2 Role play

Role B

Manchester is your home town. Use this checklist to gather information from your partner, who is a visitor.

First visit?
Impressions?
People?
Experience so far?
Likes/dislikes/preferences?
Food and wine?
Plans for the future?

12.3.1 Role play

Role A

Name:	John Davis
Company:	Conch Petroleum
Post:	Finance Manager
Born:	Sydney, Australia
Previous company:	BTE
Period with Conch:	4 years
Place of residence:	Stavanger, Norway
Married/single:	married
Children:	0
Hobbies:	reading, yachting
Future plans:	retire at 50

9.4   Role play

Role D

The growth area is in foreign markets. You think the best means of growth is through overseas agents. A new Marketing Co-ordinator should be appointed to ensure slow steady growth.

10.3   Role play

Learner B

You receive a call from A, a friend working in the same company as you, but in a different department. S/he asks you for a short chat over coffee next week. You would like to have the meeting, although you are busy. Make a note of what you decide. Today is Thursday, and this is your diary for next week.

	Morning	Afternoon
Mon.	Meeting with John R.	....
Tues.	....	....
Wed.	....	To Manchester
Thurs.	Meeting in M/c	....
Fri.	....	Phone all agents

12.3.1 Role play

Role B

Name:	Margaret Atkins
Company:	Delson Electronics
Post:	Production Manager
Born:	Denver, Colorado
Previous company:	SCT
Period with present co.:	2 years
Place of residence:	Paris
Married/single:	married
Children:	2
Hobbies:	aerobics, music
Future plans:	to set up own company

10.3 Role play

Role A

You haven't seen your partner for a long time. S/he works in the same company as you, but in a different department, and you would like to have a short meeting over coffee one day next week. Ring her/him to try to arrange this for the middle of the morning or the afternoon, in your office or your partner's. Make a note of what you decide. Today is Thursday, and this is your diary for next week.

	Morning	Afternoon
Mon.	....	Trip to London
Tues.	London	....
Wed.	....	Visit from Tom M.
Thurs.	Meeting	Factory visit
Fri.	Visit from Bill E.	

14.3.1 Role play

Role A

Your partner is visiting your home town, Salamanca, in Spain. Use the checklist to gather her/his impressions. Make a note of the information you gather.

First visit?
Impressions?
People?
Experience so far?
Likes/dislikes/preferences?
Food and wine?
Plans for the future?

Key

This key contains the answers to questions in Units 1–14. It also contains transcripts of the cassette recordings used throughout the book. It does not contain answers to the three Case Studies or to questions in the text which are purely subjective.

Unit 1

1.1.1

Features of a good presentation:

Voice – breathe slowly, control the volume
Speed – better slow than too fast; pause frequently
Language – simple short sentences; give summaries and examples
Length – people's concentration is only good for 20 minutes or so
Humour – always helps to keep your audience with you
Notes – certainly, but never read aloud a complete text
Confidence – sound as though you know what you are talking about
Visual aids – not too many; make them attractive and clear
Body language – plenty of eye contact with your audience

1.1.2

Content: clear   Delivery: clear

1.1.3

Cultural Study Tours Data Sheet

a) Glasgow
b) Edinburgh
c) limited liability company
d) 2
e) marketing
f) finance
g) 5
h) administrative
i) Great Britain, Mediterranean, E. Europe, China
j) day-to-day clerical work
k) organise tours of professional/cultural interest

Tapescript

Allan Swales: Good afternoon. My name's Allan Swales and I'd like to talk to you about my company which is called Cultural Study Tours. Basically, we offer tours in various countries including Scotland, for people who want to learn more about particular cultural aspects of those countries.

Now I thought I'd begin firstly by describing our organisation and then go on to outline for you the way in which we operate. Well, it's based in Scotland. The head office is in Glasgow but we have a small branch office in Edinburgh. It's a limited liability company, with two directors, myself and my colleague, Peter, and together we own 60% of the shares.

I'm in charge of marketing and Peter's responsible for the financial side of things. Apart from us, there are eleven full-time staff. There are five tour leaders who plan and lead the tours. Each of them is responsible for a particular region; that is Great Britain, the Russian Federation, Eastern Europe, China and the Mediterranean. The tour leaders are supported by six administrative staff who handle the day-to-day clerical work.

Now if I could give you some background to the company. We were two academics working in Glasgow University who were asked to organise a tour of Scotland for a group of visiting lecturers. That was three years ago. Since then we've developed a company which organises twenty tours a year.

Let me give you an example of a tour that we organised last year on the architecture of Hungary. Well, firstly, we set up a series of introductory lectures and visits in Budapest and then took the participants around various cities of architectural interest. The aim, therefore, was to combine a holiday with a particular professional or cultural interest.

So, what I've been trying to do this afternoon, or in this brief introduction, is to show the kind of organisation we are and the kind of tours we get involved in.

1.2.1A

1 Allan Swales	4 a limited liability company
2 Peter	5 five tour leaders
3 Glasgow	6 six administrative staff

1.2.1B   Model questions and answers

How many warehouses are there?
There are three. One in Perpignan, one in Marseille and one in Toulon.

How many sales offices are there?
There are two. One in Marseille and one in Nice.

How many R and D centres are there?
There's one. It's in Sophie Antipolis.

How many employees are there in Montpellier?
There are 75.

How many employees are there in Toulon?
There are 117 altogether. 37 in the warehouse and 80 in the factory.

1.3

Company status	public limited company partnership	
Company structure	it's made up of it's divided into	section department
People	manager staff	employee supervisor
Job description	administrative clerical	
Job function	is in charge of deals with reports to	

Unit 2

2.1.1   Model answers

1 Hello. Hi. Good to see you.
2 How do you do? Nice to meet you.
3 weather, work, where you are from

2.1.2

1 No
2 'Hello, Allan. How are you?'
3 weather, work, recent activities
4 'Peter, have you met my colleague Allan Swales. Allan this is Peter, Peter Nicholson.'
5 'How do you do?'

Tapescript

Allan   Hello, Jane, I haven't seen you for some time.
Jane   Ah hello, Allan. How are you?
Allan   Fine, thanks. How was Sweden?
Jane   Oh fine, fine. Well, you know, same as ever.
Allan   Good. Well, it's a superb day, isn't it?
Jane   Yeah, yes. Has it been like this long?
Allan   Yes, well two or three days, I think. What was the weather like in Sweden?
Jane   Great, for a change. Really good. So what have you been up to, Allan?
Allan   Well, I had a lovely weekend in the Lake District. It was really magnificent.
Jane   Yeah. And have you been working hard apart from that?
Allan   Oh yes, I'm afraid so.
Jane   Good. Anyway, come and meet a friend of mine. Peter, have you met my friend, Allan Swales, from Cultural Study Tours? Allan, this is Peter, Peter Nicholson.
Peter   How do you do?
Allan   How do you do?
Peter   So you organise tours to far-flung exotic places, do you?
Allan   Well sometimes, yes.
Peter   Good, good. Well, we're very pleased you could come and talk to us today.

2.2.1   Tapescript

A
Paul   Hello, Chris. How are you?
Chris   Fine thanks, Paul. How are you?
Paul   Very well, actually.
Chris   I haven't seen you for a while.
Paul   No, I've been busy, I'm afraid. In fact, I must be going.
Chris   OK, I'll be in touch.
Paul   Right. See you.

B

Jill	Pat, can I introduce you to Graham, Graham Murphy? Graham, this is Pat White, she's an accountant with ICN.
Graham	How do you do?
Pat	Glad to meet you.
Graham	Have you been in Montreal long?
Pat	No, I just arrived yesterday.
Graham	Great city, isn't it?
Pat	Yes, it seems really interesting.
Graham	Well, it's been nice talking to you.
Pat	Yes, nice to have met you too.

2.2.2   Tapescript

1 Greet a colleague, Paul, at work. You work in the same office.
   Hello Paul, how are things?
2 You meet a business visitor, Julie, at the airport. Greet her and start a conversation.
   Nice to see you again, Julie. How was your trip?
3 You are talking to someone you have just met at a conference. Close the conversation politely.
   Well, it was very interesting talking to you. I hope I see you again sometime.
4 You see a good friend of yours, Frank, in the staff canteen. He has just got back from a business trip. Greet him and start a conversation.
   Frank! You're back. How was the trip?
5 Introduce a business visitor, Joanne Lane from Montreal, to one of your colleagues, Jack.
   Jack, I don't think you've met Joanne, Joanne Lane from Montreal.

Unit 3

3.1.2

Clive Farmer agrees with the more modern view of quality as 'the ability of a service or product to satisfy a given need'.

3.1.3

A

Area	Order
Describing visual information	4
Defining the company's aims	3
Describing his job	1
Calculating quality costs	2

3.1.3   B   He explains very clearly.

The aim is to get people to repurchase all of our products as often as they possibly can and to prefer them to our competitors' products, so they'll buy more of ours and less of theirs, in such a way as to make a profit.

3.1.3   C   He describes the graph clearly.

a   number of defects

b   investment in prevention of defects

Tapescript

Julie Robson: So, if you can maybe tell me a little about what you've been doing since you joined the company – when was it?

Clive Farmer: Yeah, I joined Rowburys in 86 as the company Quality Services Manager – er – I think that – um – Rowburys at the time had a fairly traditional view of quality which tended to be associated with – um – excellence – rather than a rather more modern quality view which is to do with the total quality of business – and – how quality fits into its market place – and quality costs and so I tried to change that awareness.

Julie Robson: So, what are the aims of – er – your company in terms of quality? What are you aiming at?

Clive Farmer: The aim is to get people to repurchase all of our products as often as they possibly can and to prefer them to our competitors' products, so they'll buy more of ours and less of theirs – er – in such a way as to make a profit – I mean we're actually about making a profit more than anything else.

Julie Robson: Yeah, yes.

Clive Farmer: But of course if you're going to do that – then you have to know what you're doing in quality it's, it's – got to be a cold-blooded thing – and you have to manage and control quality – and that's from the top of the business to the bottom of the business. And then – what you can do – is look at an optimum quality cost model, again, to look – to see how you should achieve quality.

Julie Robson: So what does this graph actually represent?

Clive Farmer: Well, this, it's, it's an Optimum Quality Cost Model which shows that – on one axis it's showing the cost of actually making the product and the other axis is the reducing number of defects – or, or it's the percentage of the products – er – that is defective, which we can use as a measure of quality (so going from 100%) – yeah – yeah – you go from 100% down to zero. So, when you start off, if you've got one heck of a lot of failures – er – then you

would have very, very high failure costs (right) – right –
and, and very low prevention costs, because you're not
actually spending any money preventing anything. And
gradually – as you invest some money in prevention costs,
then you get a dramatic fall in the percentage that you get
of defects. Therefore, the failure costs go down very
steeply. (OK) But gradually, of course, these two start to
overtake each other – and there becomes a cross-over
point where – if you invest any more money – at that
point – actually going beyond there – is costing the
business money, and, obviously, at that point where
you've invested exactly the amount of money that you
needed to invest – in order to maximise the amount of
prevention – at that point, it's going to be the lowest cost
for that unit.

3.2.1   Model answer

Market research is the investigation of the needs and potential of a market.	Define
It includes the definition of objectives, the collection and analysis of results and the presentation of findings.	Describe
A company may use market research to decide on demand for a product.	Illustrate
Market research enables companies to make informed decisions about marketing strategy and its implementation.	Rephrase

3.2.3

a, d a sharp fall/a steep drop
b   a levelling-off/a stable period
c, e a dramatic rise/a sudden increase

3.2.4

1 As you can see in the graph, costs fell dramatically in the first two
   months.
2 In March, costs continued to drop but more gradually.
3 Costs fell from 15m to 12m during this period.
4 During the next one and a half months there was a levelling-off of
   costs.
5 However, in mid May they rose to 25m.
6 In June they continued to rise but more slowly, from 25m to 28m.
7 In the next two months costs dropped again steeply to 12m.
8 However, the trend changed in September when costs increased
   dramatically to 32m.

3.2.5 Model description of the bar chart

In Belgium the working week fell from $42\frac{1}{2}$ hours to $32\frac{1}{2}$ hours.
In France the number of hours worked per person dropped by $7\frac{1}{2}$ hours
per week to $32\frac{1}{2}$ hours.
Japan and the USA reduced their working week by 4 hours.
In Germany and Hong Kong the number of hours worked per week fell
by two.
Britain showed the least change over the period; the working week
decreased by 1 hour to 34 hours per week.

3.3.1

Nouns	Verbs
MAXimum	to MAXimise
OPtimum	to OPtimise
STANdard	to STANdardise
aCHIEVement	to aCHIEVE
preVENtion	to preVENT
aim	to aim
sucCESS	to sucCEED
FAIlure	to fail
MANagement	to MANage
conTROL	to conTROL
calcuLAtion	to CALculate
MEAsurement	to MEAsure
reDUCtion	to reDUCE
inVESTment	to inVEST

3.3.2 Tapescript

1 a We need to maximise our production capacity.
  b We must reach maximum capacity.
2 a Our optimum sales target is 15.5 million.
  b We could optimise sales at 15.5 million.
3 a Their products don't meet European standards.
  b They must standardise their products in line with Europe.
4 a The economy achieved 6% real growth last year.
  b 6% growth rate is quite an economic achievement.
5 a All our staff must do fire prevention training.
  b We give regular staff training to prevent fire.
6 a Our aim in the next six months is to cut down on unnecessary
    expenditure.
  b We aim to reduce unnecessary expenses.
7 a The computer's down because of a power failure.
  b The power has failed again, so the computer's down.
8 a Can you manage the office on your own while I'm in Geneva?
  b The office management will be your responsibility while I'm
    away.

9 a Quality control is an important part of our production process.
   b We use several tests to control quality.
10 a According to your calculations we've overrun the budget.
    b You calculate that we've overspent the budget.
11 a We can use the Optimum Quality Cost Model to measure quality.
    b This model is used as a measurement of quality.
12 a We must invest more money in R & D.
    b We must increase investment in R & D.
13 a If we spend more on prevention costs, we will reduce failures.
    b Increasing prevention costs will result in a reduction of failures.

Unit 4

4.1.1   Model answers

a) Hello. Could I speak to ...?
b) Hello. Paul Wong speaking.

Photos:

a) Good morning, Allied Products. Can I help you?
b) Michel Brecht speaking.
c) Hello. Could I speak to David, please?

4.1.2

1 false; 2 true; 3 false; 4 true; 5 false; 6 true

4.1.3

1 OK. Goodbye then. e)
2 What can I do for you? b)
3 I think I left a file in your office. c)
4 Hello, Dr Farmer. This is Julie Robson. a)
5 You remember I interviewed you? b)
6 Thanks again for your time. d)
7 Would you mind putting it in the post? c)
8 Don't mention it. I enjoyed it. d)

Tapescript

Switchboard: Good morning. Rowburys.
Julie Robson: Good morning. Could you put me through to Clive Farmer's office?
Switchboard: Who's calling, please?
Julie Robson: Julie Robson.
Switchboard: One moment. I'll put you through
Clive Farmer: Clive Farmer speaking.
Julie Robson: Oh, hello, Dr Farmer. This is Julie Robson here. You remember I interviewed you on Friday?
Clive Farmer: Oh, yes, yes. Hello, Julie. What can I do for you?
Julie Robson: I think I left a file in your office last week. It's a white binder with my name on.
Clive Farmer: Hang on a moment. Yes. Ms J. Robson.
Julie Robson: Oh, good. Would you mind putting it in the post for me?
Clive Farmer: Not at all. I'll do that today.
Julie Robson: Thanks very much. Sorry to be a nuisance. And thanks again for your time on Friday, it was very useful.
Clive Farmer: Don't mention it. I enjoyed it.
Julie Robson: OK. Goodbye then.
Clive Farmer: Goodbye.

4.2.1   Tapescript

A

Receptionist: Tudor Hotel. Good morning.
Caller: Could I speak to Mr Clayton, please?
Receptionist: Who's calling, please?
Caller: This is Chris Jones.
Receptionist: Right, Mr Jones, I'll put you through.
Caller: Thank you.

B

Mrs Thomas: Hello, 652 011.
Jack: Hello. Could I speak to Diane, please? This is Jack.
Mrs Thomas: Hello, Jack. How are you?
Jack: Fine thanks, Mrs Thomas.
Mrs Thomas: I'm sorry, Diane's not in.
Jack: Could you give her a message?
Mrs Thomas: Yes, of course.
Jack: I'm phoning about the party this evening. What time shall I pick her up? Will you ask her to phone me?
Mrs Thomas: Right. I'll give her the message.
Jack: Thanks. Bye.
Mrs Thomas: Goodbye.

Unit 5

5.1.1

At a trade fair people exchange information about: products, product ranges, prices, availability, new technology.

5.1.2   Golf Pro

Product range	Price
Metal woods	£90–£149 each
Golf Pro Ladies (set)	£465
Woods (set)	£240
Putters	£46 each
Golf Pro (set)	£835

Tapescript

Hubert: Good morning.

Usugi: Good morning.

Hubert: Can I help you?

Usugi: Er, thank you but I'm just looking at the moment.

Hubert: Yes, please do. Have you come across our products before?

Usugi: I think I have heard of them, yes.

Hubert: We are relatively new but Golf Pro is acquiring a reputation very quickly. We have become world leaders in metal woods.

Usugi: Really? Well, actually I am quite interested in metal woods. Could you tell me what the prices are in this range?

Hubert: Of course. The prices start at £90 and they go up to £149.

Usugi: Did you say £149?

Hubert: Yes, that's right. I wonder if you would be interested in our new range of ladies' clubs as well?

Usugi: Well, possibly. Do you think you could give me the prices?

Hubert: Yes. The range is called Golf Pro Lady and the full set of nine irons comes to £465. Woods, the set of three is £240 and putters are £46 each.

Usugi: So, that was £46 each, wasn't it?

Hubert: Yes, £46 each.

Usugi: Right, thank you, do you have some information about your top of the range full set of clubs as well?

Hubert: Of course. That is our Golf Pro X. This is real state-of-the-art when it comes to professional clubs. The set of nine irons comes to £835. Very reasonable I think you'll agree.

Usugi: Mmm, not bad.

Hubert: Would you like to try one out in the practice area?

Usugi: Er, no thank you. I'm afraid I don't have time at the moment. But I would like to read some more about your products.

Hubert: Of course. Here are some of our latest brochures with up-to-date information on the full ranges. And also my card.

Usugi: Thank you.

Hubert: Please contact me if you need any more information.

5.1.3

a) relatively new   e) range
b) acquiring   f) Prices
c) reputation   g) up-to-date
d) world leaders   h) latest

5.2.2

1 a) Can I help you at all?
   b) I'm just looking thanks.
2 a) Have you heard of our products before?
   b) No, I don't think so.
3 a) How much are the metal woods?
   b) £85 each.
4 a) Does the price include VAT?
   b) No, I'm afraid it doesn't.
5 a) Can you tell me the price range for putters?
   b) Certainly, prices start at about £35.
6 a) That was £35, wasn't it?
   b) Yes, that's right.

5.2.3   Tapescript

Salesperson: Can I help you?

Customer: Could you give me some information about rail systems for audio visual equipment?

Salesperson: Certainly, here's our brochure.

Customer: Thank you.

Salesperson: There are two types of rail. The standard type here in plain metal.

Customer: I really wanted white.

Salesperson: Ah. Then the deluxe rail comes in ten different colours, including white.

Customer: Are there different sizes?

Salesperson: The width doesn't vary but you can order any length you want.

Customer: The price includes delivery and installation, doesn't it?

Salesperson: Yes, it does.

Customer: Do you supply the accessories for attaching the equipment?

Salesperson: Yes, the full range of accessories is described in the brochure.

Customer: Well, thank you very much.

5.3.1

a 5; b 8; c 4; d 7; e 1; f 6; g 3; h 2

a -- . . --
top of the range
b -- . . --
state of the art
c -- . --
up-to-date
d -- . --
out of date
e -- . ----
up to scratch
f -- . . -- .
out of production
g --. -- --
in the pipeline
h -- . . --
first in the field

Unit 6

6.1.1

The *venue, holidays, current affairs* and *food* are good general topics that most people are interested in.
Sex, religion and *politics* are traditionally *taboo*.

6.1.2

1 false; 2 true; 3 false; 4 false; 5 false; 6 false

Tapescript

Genevieve: Hello again, Jane. Thank goodness that's it for today. How are things going?

Jane: Hello, Genevieve. Oh, it's been incredibly busy today.

Genevieve: Would you like a drink? What can I get you?

Jane: Oh, I'd love one, please. A mineral water?

Genevieve: OK.

Brian: Hello, Jane.

Jane: Hi.

Brian: How are you doing?

Jane: OK. Oh, thank you, Genevieve. That's great. Genevieve, this is my colleague, Brian. Genevieve's on the Golf Pro stand.

Brian: Hi.

Genevieve: Hello, Brian. Nice to meet you. This bar is so busy this evening.

Brian: Yeah.

Jane: Yes. It's always like this on a first night. Don't worry, it'll be quieter tomorrow.

Genevieve: Oh, I'm going tomorrow lunchtime.

Brian: Really. Where're you going?

Genevieve: I'm going to visit a supplier in Scotland. Near St Andrews.

Brian: Great. That's the place to sell golf clubs. Terrific golf course there.

Genevieve: Yes. I managed a round on my last trip there but I won't tell you my score.

Brian: Oh, you play ...

6.2.1 Model dialogue

A Did you take a holiday last year?

B Yes. We went on one of those activity holidays in the Pyrenees.

A Sounds interesting.

B Yes, it was very good. So well-organised and not expensive.

A Really?

B Yes. It's difficult to find a holiday to suit all the family.

A Of course.

B Personally, I like to get away from people.

A Mmm. Me too.

B But the children prefer lots of organised activity.

A Sure.

B We may do the same sort of thing but in Greece this year.

A That would be nice.

B I've always liked the idea of a watersports holiday.

A Sounds good.

B What about yourself? What did you do last year?

6.2.2

terRIFic	terRIFically
aMAZing	aMAZingly
inCREdible	inCREdibly
fanTAStic	fanTAStically

6.2.3 Model dialogue

A We went to see that new film last night.
B Oh, what was it like?
A **Incredibly** funny.
B Mmm.
A Then we went to the Thai restaurant for a meal.
B Oh really, was it good?
A It was **great**.
B Yes?
A **Really** friendly atmosphere. **Fantastic** service.
B What about the food?
A **Terrific**. Try it yourself sometime.
B Maybe. It's a bit pricey though, isn't it?
A No, actually, it's **amazingly** cheap.

Unit 7

7.1.1

1 manufacturing, administration, reception, storage, research.
2 to meet suppliers; to build customer/client relations; to check out production capacity; to inspect quality.
3 questions about size and capacity of the factory, number of employees, history of the company, percentage of exports.

7.1.2

a) packaging	b) 150,000	c) one third	d) 40%
e) 29bn lira	f) medical drugs	g) 1971	h) computerised
i) automated	j) up-to-date		

Tapescript

Balazzo: How do you do, Mr Williams? Welcome to Vicenza and to Flexipak.

Williams: How do you do, Mr Balazzo?

Balazzo: Did you have a good flight?

Williams: It wasn't too bad. It was a bit full and crowded but, er, the flight was on time.

Balazzo: Good. You've been to Italy before, haven't you?

Williams: Yes, yes, I've been here once before. On holiday in Rome.

Balazzo: Rome! A beautiful city (yes indeed). Er, how was the weather in Glasgow?

Williams: Well, you won't be surprised to hear that it was raining when I left. A bit different from here!

Balazzo: Uh, yes it's been quite pleasant recently. Er, how long are you going to be in Italy?

Williams: I expect to be here for three days.

Balazzo: Good, good. Well, I suggest we go to my office and continue our conversation there. It's just down the corridor here.

Balazzo: Mr Williams, I will show you round the factory afterwards but first of all I would like to give you a brief introduction to the company.

Williams: Thank you.

Balazzo: Here in the brochure is a photograph of the plant.

Williams: Right.

Balazzo: Here you can see the main plant on this page. The production unit covers 150,000 square metres. Now, one third of this area is for the storage of raw materials and finished products. Two thirds is the factory building itself.

Williams: Yes, yes I see. It looks very impressive.

Balazzo: Thank you.

Williams: And, er, how much of your total production do you export?

Balazzo: Well, we export about 40% of total production. Last year we had a turnover of 29bn lira. Now let me show you a sample of our product. As you can see, it is, er, really multi-layer packaging. Laminates, in other words, of various materials such as plastic film, aluminium foil and paper. Now this is all used for foodstuffs, such as biscuits, coffee, even chewing gum and also medical drugs like aspirin.

Williams: Yes, well that's very interesting. It's the sort of packaging we might be looking for.

Balazzo: Really. Well, now, shall we have a walk around? First we can visit the main section of our production processes and, er, go on through the warehouse and to finish with we can visit the quality control lab.

Williams: Mm, well your warehouse certainly seems very modern and efficient.

Balazzo: Er, yes we hope so. Er, the factory of course was completed in 1981. The warehouse is, as you can see, highly automated with a computerised stock control system. And, er, automated sorting of course (yes, yes). We, we use bar codes.

Williams: Right.

Balazzo: And here is our quality control lab.

Williams: Yes, I see. Er, how long has your company been working in this field?

Balazzo: Since, er, 1971, when the company was established by my brother. We of course use the most up-to-date checking instruments to ensure products meet international standards. Also, we are doing research into new production methods.

Williams: Really.

Balazzo: Well, Mr Williams, it's nearly one o'clock so I would be pleased if you would have lunch with me in the staff restaurant.

Williams: Oh, that would be a pleasure.

Balazzo: And we can continue our conversation there.

Williams: Thank you.

7.1.3

1 How do you do, Mr Williams? Welcome to Vicenza and to Flexipak.
2 Shall we have a walk around?
3 Here you can see the main plant.
   And here is our quality control lab.
4 Right.
   Yes, I see. It looks very impressive.
   Yes, well that's very interesting.

7.2.2   Model answer

When an order is placed, the order department checks with the warehouse to see if the item is in stock. If it is not, the customer is informed immediately. If it is in stock, the order is passed to dispatch for delivery. On delivery, the customer signs the delivery note and this is returned to accounts. An invoice is then sent to the customer for payment for the goods received.

7.3.1 Tapescript

1 multi-layer packaging
2 computerised stock control system
3 quality control lab
4 up-to-date checking instruments
5 new production methods
6 automated sorting system

Unit 8

8.1.2

1 false; 2 true; 3 false; 4 true; 5 false

Tapescript

Balazzo: I reserved this table. I thought it would be very pleasant to sit by the window.

Williams: Yes indeed, thank you. It's a very nice restaurant.

Balazzo: Now, here's the menu. Would you like me to recommend something?

Williams: I think that would be a good idea. I'm afraid my Italian isn't very good.

Balazzo: (laugh) Well now let me see, er, *insalata caprese* is mixed salad consisting of mozzarella cheese and tomatoes, *vongole* is seafood and *pollo* is chicken.

Williams: Ah well, yes, I'd quite like to have *pollo venezia* and some salad.

Balazzo: Right. I think I'll have the same.

Balazzo: Well, I hope you enjoyed your meal.

Williams: Oh, absolutely delicious.

Balazzo: Good. Now this evening, as I mentioned, I will have the pleasure, I hope, of taking you out for dinner at the very famous restaurant in Vicenza called the San Lorenzo.

Williams: That would be wonderful.

Balazzo: Let me pick you up from your hotel at eight o'clock.

Williams: Yeah, that's fine. Thank you.

Balazzo: Good. Well, I believe you're meeting my colleague Senora Grotto after lunch.

Williams: Yes, that's right.

Balazzo: At what time?

Williams: Well, our appointment's for two o'clock.

Balazzo: Right. Well, I'll take you to Senora Grotto's office. It's on the fourth floor.

Williams: Thank you.

Balazzo: My pleasure.

8.1.3

1 Would you like me to recommend something?
2 I'd quite like to have *pollo venezia*.
3 I hope you enjoyed your meal.
4 Let me pick you up from your hotel at eight o'clock.
5 I'll take you to Senora Grotto's office.

8.2.1 Model dialogue

A Here's the menu, Mr Clarke.
B Thank you. Goodness, it's all in Greek!
A Yes, I'm afraid so. **Would you like me to** recommend something?
B **That would be very nice,** thank you.
A Well, let's see. There's *dolmades*, that's vine leaves stuffed with spiced meat.
B That sounds nice.
A By the way, before I forget, **I'd like to invite you** to dinner at my home this evening, if you're free?
B **That would be delightful,** thank you very much.

8.2.2 **Tapescript**

a) Can I get you a drink?
   (That would be very nice.)
b) I'll give you a lift to your hotel.
   (Thank you, that's very kind of you.)
c) Would you like me to recommend something on the menu?
   (Yes, I'd like that very much.)
d) Would you like me to get you a taxi?
   (Yes please, if it's no bother.)
e) Can I invite you to dinner this evening?
   (That would be delightful, thank you.)

Unit 9

9.1.2

1 2,560
2 memos, questionnaires, instructions, up-dates, letters, reports, surveys
3 720
4 change from paper to face-to-face
5 more meetings, video-conferencing
6 it's too easy; it creates paper

9.1.3

1 I think the vital thing to point out is …
2 I have always understood …
3 I agree, Peter. It has …
4 We feel that …
5 Don't you think …?
6 I can't agree with you.
7 In my view …

Tapescript

Klaus Ehlers:	OK, first of all … er, could I ask if anyone has any questions, er, on this survey the working party has carried out in the Madrid office?
Andrea Thompson:	Er, yes. Can I just check the figures? Were there really 2,560 sheets in one month?
Klaus Ehlers:	Oh yes, absolutely. They were carefully counted.
Andrea Thompson:	Could you say what sort of papers they were?
Klaus Ehlers:	Er, well, they varied. There were memos, questionnaires, instructions, up-dates, letters, reports, surveys. All kinds of paperwork.
Mariluz Rivera:	Yes, it's quite true there were over two and a half thousand sheets of paper. But before we begin our discussion, Klaus, I think the vital thing to point out is the number of copies included in that figure. In fact there were 720 original sheets, the rest were copies.
Peter Wang:	It seems a fantastic amount of paper, but I have always understood that company policy stressed the importance of internal communications.
Klaus Ehlers:	I agree, Peter. It has. But we must find a balance which is practicable. Madrid is clearly drowning under a sea of paper.
Andrea Thompson:	So what recommendations has the working party come up with?
Klaus Ehlers:	We feel that the emphasis should be moved to face-to-face communication. Departmental managers should be encouraged to hold more meetings. Video-conferencing could also be more widely used between branches and subsidiaries. This would radically cut the number of fourth and fifth copies in circulation.
Peter Wang:	Don't you think this would be expensive? Especially for routine messages. Why not use fax?
Mariluz Rivera:	But excuse me, Peter. I can't agree with you. They just create more paper. In my view it's since the wide use of fax machines that the paper problem has got out of hand. It's too easy …

9.2.1

A 1 agreeing; 2 stating; 3 agreeing; 4 disagreeing; 5 disagreeing; 6 agreeing

Model answers

B 1 I can't agree with you there.
2 I quite agree.
3 I couldn't agree more.
4 I'm not at all sure.
5 I disagree. I think we have too many.
6 I agree. It is.

9.2.2

1 We publish a newsletter three times a year.
2 We phone New York three times a day.
3 We contact the warehouse every other week.
4 We use electronic mail every day.
5 We pay 50 pence per A4 sheet for the use of the fax.
6 We receive a circular twice a week.

9.3.1

1 memo; 2 electronic mail; 3 report; 4 telephone conference; 5 brochure

9.3.2

1) fax; 2) questionnaire; 3) video conference; 4) letter; 5) survey; 6) memo

Unit 10

10.1.2

1 Madrid; 2 London; 3 Birmingham; 4 April 19th–23rd; 5 Tom Gibson; 6 London; 7 Friday April 23rd; 8 12.30; 9 lunch

Tapescript

Andrea Thompson: Andrea Thompson speaking.
Mariluz Rivera: Hello, Andrea, this is Mariluz Rivera from Madrid. How are you?
Andrea Thompson: Mariluz! How nice to hear from you. I'm fine, thanks, how are you?

Mariluz Rivera:	Fine. Look, I'm coming over in April for the conference in Birmingham. Are you going?
Andrea Thompson:	No, not this year. You know Tom Gibson, from Personnel? He's going this year.
Mariluz Rivera:	Sorry, what was that? The line's not too good. I couldn't hear you.
Andrea Thompson:	I said, unfortunately no. Tom Gibson from Personnel is going this year.
Mariluz Rivera:	What a shame! So I won't see you there. How about meeting in London on my way through? I can get an earlier flight. That would be on the 19th.
Andrea Thompson:	Just a minute, I'll check my diary. No, I'm afraid it's no good, I'm in Manchester all day. What about after the conference, on your way home?
Mariluz Rivera:	Yes, that's possible. On Friday the 23rd, then?
Andrea Thompson:	Yes. Would you like to meet for lunch?
Mariluz Rivera:	Good idea. I suggest that I come and meet you at the bank.
Andrea Thompson:	OK, let's say 12.30. If you get delayed, you can always ring me.
Mariluz Rivera:	Great. So, see you at your office at 12.30 on the 23rd.
Andrea Thompson:	Wonderful. See you then. Thanks for phoning, Mariluz. Bye. Bye.

10.2.1 Model answers

1 A How about a game of tennis on Saturday?
  B Saturday's no good. What about Sunday?
2 A Would you like to go out to a restaurant on Friday evening?
  B Yes, I'd love to. Let's try the new Mexican place.
3 A What about going to a football match at the weekend?
  B Yes, great. Let's get tickets for the game on Saturday.
4 A Can you come to the cinema tonight?
  B I'm afraid tonight's no good. How about tomorrow?
5 A How about a drink after work?
  B OK. I'll see you in the bar at 6.30.

10.2.2

1 tomorrow at 6 p.m.
2 at the weekend, or on Monday
3 tonight
4 in winter, in summer
5 in the 18th century
6 in 1995
7 last night, at midnight
8 at Christmas
9 next Wednesday, in the evening
10 tomorrow, at 9 o'clock
11 at the moment, at 2 o'clock
12 on Wednesday, the 8th of May, at 11.30 in the morning

10.2.**3**   **Tapescript**

A David Unwin speaking.
B Hello, David, this is Elisabeth Hollins from Conway Communications.
A Hello, Elisabeth, how are you?
B Fine thanks, how about you?
A Not too bad. Very busy, as usual.
B Look, David, I'm ringing to see if we can arrange a time for a meeting to discuss your new publicity campaign.
A Fine. What time were you thinking of?
B How about next Wednesday, the 10th?
A I'm afraid that's not too good for me; I have a meeting. Does Monday the 8th suit you?
B Yes, that's fine. What time suits you best?
A Is 9 o'clock OK for you?
B Yes, that's fine by me. Shall we meet in your office or mine?
A Let's make it my place; then you can talk to my people about your ideas.
B Fine, David. So that's next Monday, the 8th, in your office?
A That's right. I look forward to seeing you then, Elisabeth.
B Me too. Bye, David.
A Bye, Elisabeth. Thanks for ringing.

Unit 11

11.1.**1**

number; discounts for quantity; delivery time; quality of product or service; specifications; service and maintenance; freight charges; insurance.

11.1.**2**

1) 20 cents per unit; 2) 20 cents; 3) 750,000; 4) 1m at 15 cents; 5) 30 days; 6) faulty cards; 7) visit the factory

Tapescript

Bill Klyne: Well, Ed, how are things in the banking world?
Ed Murray: Oh, fine. Pretty good really.
Bill Klyne: Good, good. Well, look, what I've come to talk to you about is your plastic card order for next year.
Ed Murray: Uh huh.

Bill Klyne: It's my guess you'll need more cards for next year, right?
Ed Murray: Well, maybe er ... It really depends on the price.
Bill Klyne: OK. I've got to tell you straight that we have had to increase prices a little because of inflation ... cost of raw materials, but we do have an improved product.
Ed Murray: Well, I don't know, Bill. Price is a very crucial factor in our business.
Bill Klyne: I understand that. Er, I can keep the price at the same level if you can increase the number of cards you're ordering from us.
Ed Murray: OK. Well, what number are we talking about?
Bill Klyne: We'd have to go up to about 700,000. Then we could keep the unit price at 20 cents. How's that?
Ed Murray: Wait a minute, Bill. 20 cents a unit. You'll have to do better than that. If I remember correctly, the unit price last year was 18 cents.
Bill Klyne: Look, Ed. I'll tell you what I'll do. If you can get in an order of 750,000 by the end of the month, I can discount it to 18 cents a unit. Order a million and you can have them for 15 cents. How about that?
Ed Murray: I'll think about that, Bill. And what about delivery?
Bill Klyne: The usual 30 day service. We can get a million cards through to you in 30 days.
Ed Murray: Well, I dunno Bill, before we go ahead and order there are a couple of things I'd like to bring up. Around 3% of last year's cards were faulty you know.
Bill Klyne: I'll look into that, Ed, but you know our quality control has been revolutionised. Why don't you come down and see for yourself?
Ed Murray: Can I get back to you on that one? You know it's ...

11.1.3   1–b; 2–f; 3–e; 4–a; 5–d; 6–c

Tapescript

1 I would like to mention a couple of things here, Bill, the quality and the packaging of the product.
2 And what about the question of rising prices?
3 I'd like to mention that we weren't too happy with delivery times.
4 Look, what I wanted to talk to you about was this problem of delivery.
5 I tell you what, why not try something different?
6 I've got to tell you straight, this just isn't good enough.

11.2.1

1 If the parts arrive on time, production will start immediately.
2 If you call tomorrow, I will have time to talk.
3 If you increase the order, I will lower the price.
4 If we don't leave soon, we will arrive too late.
5 If we take quality control seriously, standards will improve.
6 If they promise to deliver on time, we can be sure they will.
7 If you tell me your arrival time, I will meet you at the airport.

11.2.2 Model answers

1 I'll look into that straight away.
2 Wait a minute …
3 I'll have to think about that.
4 It's difficult to say at the moment.
5 Well, maybe. It really depends on the price.
6 Can I get back to you on that one?

11.3.1

1 manufacture/production; 2 retailer; 3 sub-contractor;
4 distribution/delivery; 5 purchaser; 6 factory/plant

11.3.2

1 are manufactured; 2 buys; 3 are stored/kept; 4 sells; 5 are distributed;
6 supplies; 7 are delivered

Unit 12

12.1.2

1 about 8 years ago; 2 investment; 3 Bill – Philadelphia; Ed – Richmond,
Virginia; 4 Yes, a wife and two children; 5 divorced; 6 Yes, two boys;
7 golf; 8 a golf tournament; 9 he's going to Colorado

Tapescript

Bill Klyne: You know, Ed, I'm really glad you could make this trip to
Washington. I appreciate being able to show you round.
Ed Murray: Well, I have a meeting in town later today so it seemed a
good idea.
Bill Klyne: So how long have you been with Baltimore City Bank now,
Ed?

Ed Murray: Um ... I guess I joined about 8 years ago. First I was in investment, then I moved to purchasing five years ago.

Bill Klyne: Oh, so the Stock Market got a bit hot for you, eh?

Ed Murray: No, it's not like that in Baltimore – quite the opposite. Wall Street is where it's all happening in investments. But purchasing is great: lots of people to meet, lots of travel, hard talking, decent hours. How about you, Bill? Have you always been in the 'plastic revolution' business?

Bill Klyne: No, not always. I sold a lot of things before plastic cards.

Ed Murray: Do you come from these parts?

Bill Klyne: Well, I was born in Philadelphia, but I moved here as a kid. How about you? Where are you from?

Ed Murray: Richmond, Virginia's my home town. I moved to Baltimore 20 years ago when I got married and had my first job. Do you have a family?

Bill Klyne: Yeah, my wife Kitty, and two kids at High School. We live just outside town. How about you?

Ed Murray: Mm. Two boys at college. They live with their mother – we're divorced. Plenty of time for my golf!

Bill Klyne: Golf! Hey, that's great! How about a round of golf out here one weekend? We have some great courses here in Washington.

Ed Murray: I'd like that. But we're having a sort of tournament in Baltimore next weekend. Why not come along and join us?

Bill Klyne: Uh uh, 'fraid not, Ed. My wife and I have planned a trip to Colorado; so we'll be walking through the trees not over the greens.

12.2.1

1 I have a meeting in town later today.
2 Purchasing is great.
3 Richmond, Virginia's my home town.
4 We live just outside town.
5 They live with their mother.
6 I moved to purchasing five years ago.
7 I sold a lot of things before plastic cards.
8 I was born in Philadelphia.
9 I moved here as a kid.
10 My wife and I have planned a trip to Colorado.
11 Have you always been in the plastic revolution business?
12 We'll be walking through the trees ...

Unit 13

13.1.**1**

Some chairperson duties: guide the discussion, move through the agenda, control the discussion, summarise points, minute decisions, bring people in, end the meeting.

13.1.**2**

1 False; 2 True; 3 True; 4 True; 5 False; 6 True

13.1.**3**

4 He calls the meeting to order.
6 He establishes the tone.
1 He invites Mr Banks to speak.
5 He asks someone to introduce the second item on the agenda.
2 He calls for a decision to be minuted.
3 He asks for comment on Item 3.
7 He moves on to the next item.

Tapescript

Rafael González:	So, perhaps we could call our meeting to order. Um...Before we begin I should like to say that I hope the meeting will be constructive and have a positive outcome. The purpose is to resolve a few problems which have been caused by the recent merger of our two companies. Perhaps I could start by asking Mr Banks for a few words?
John Banks:	Sure. I share Sr González's hopes for a constructive meeting. I also hope that some ways will be found for working a little more closely together than we have up to now and therefore getting better results both for us at Delco and for you at Duo.
Maggie Seabrook:	Agreed.
Rafael González:	Right. May we move on to the agenda then, please?
John Banks:	Right.
Rafael González:	Teresa, could, could you please start for us?
Teresa Navarro:	Well, on the question of financial control, it seems to us in Spain that Duo has lost all its power in financial matters and we now have to get permission from Delco for the smallest expenditure.
Maggie Seabrook:	I can't agree, Miss Navarro. This is not an accurate picture. The position is that we have two different types of financial management ... the American financial management and the Spanish financial

	management. Our objective should be to take the best of both.
John Banks:	I agree with Miss Seabrook entirely. Could I suggest the formation of a working party for closer examination of the two systems?
Rafael González:	This seems a sensible and constructive suggestion. Who agrees with forming a working party?
Teresa Navarro:	Mmm.
Maggie Seabrook:	Yes. Good idea.
Rafael González:	All right. Let's, let's do this. We'll note this in a minute and move on to the next item on the agenda, Production planning. Who would like to start with a comment on this?
Teresa Navarro:	There's no one here from Production.
Rafael González:	Right. Does anyone object if we leave this for now and move on to Personnel?
All:	Fine/sure.
Rafael González:	So, who would like to start?
Teresa Navarro:	I'd like to put Duo's point of view to the meeting. Our Human Resources Manager is unable to be present today but he asked me to explain how so many Spanish employees are worried and upset about the rapid changes ...

13.2   Model answers

1 So who would like to start with comments on the new training plan?
2 Why don't we leave this for now?
3 Can we move on to this year's figures?
4 Before we begin, I should like to say that I hope this meeting will be a brief but friendly one.
5 Elizabeth, would you like to say something here about our information policy?
6 So, perhaps we could call our budget meeting to order?
7 Our position seems to be that we all agree that something must be done immediately.

13.3.1

1–d; 2–e; 3–a; 4–b; 5–c; 6–i; 7–h; 8–g; 9–j; 10–f

Unit 14

14.1.2 1 tapas; 2 Granada; 3 the Prado; 4 Fallas in Valencia; 5 seafood;
6 the Alhambra; 7 the Retiro

Tapescript

Rafael González: Is this your first visit to Madrid?

Maggie Seabrook: No. Twenty years ago I spent some time in Europe
and Madrid was my first stop. It was quite a culture
shock then, I can tell you. New York a few hours
before, then this beautiful old city with all its history.

Rafael González: Do you think it has changed?

Maggie Seabrook: Actually, not really. More traffic I guess.

Rafael González: Have you had the opportunity to be a tourist this
time?

Maggie Seabrook: Well, I managed an hour in the Prado yesterday and
I've walked around quite a bit; the park – the Retiro,
and the old city. Ah, I love it.

Rafael González: Good, good, and what about our Spanish food?

Maggie Seabrook: Oh, great. All those little dishes in the bars.

Rafael González: Ah, the *tapas*.

Maggie Seabrook: Yes. And the seafood is marvellous.

Rafael González: We are fortunate, the seafood in Madrid is excellent.
What other parts of Spain have you seen?

Maggie Seabrook: I'll never forget Granada. Those rooftops. And the
palace there – what's it called?

Rafael González: The Alhambra.

Maggie Seabrook: Yeah. We don't have anything like that in the States.
Then I spent some time in Valencia. That was great.
The city was so colourful with all those huge models
they make.

Rafael González: Oh, you must have been there in March for *Fallas*.

Maggie Seabrook: Yeah. That was fun. Are you from Madrid, Rafael?

Rafael González: No. No, actually my home is near Valencia. The little
town of Alcoy. We have a wonderful festival in spring
there too. The whole town replays the battle for
Spain between the Christians and the Moors.

Maggie Seabrook: Saint George and all that. Yes, I remember reading
about it. I'd love to see it some day.

Rafael González: Did you visit any of our beaches?

Maggie Seabrook: Only at Valencia. It was too early in the year really.
We took the train up to Barcelona then and on into
France. I'd love to come back for a holiday with my
husband …

14.1.3

1 Is this your first visit to Madrid?
2 Do you think it has changed?
3 Have you had the opportunity to be a tourist this time?
4 And what about our Spanish food?
5 What other parts of Spain have you seen?
6 Did you visit any of our beaches? (i.e. 20 years ago)

14.2.1

1 What do you think of York?
d It's a lovely place.
2 How do you find the people?
g They're very friendly.
3 Have you been here before?
a No, it's my first visit.
4 Have you visited the Minster?
c Yes, I have, it's wonderful.
5 What do you like best?
b I love the old streets.
6 What do you think of the restaurants?
f They're OK – a bit traditional.
7 What are your plans?
e I'd like to see the countryside.